ABCs of Building
MODEL RAILROAD CARS

To our sons, Tony and Steven

ABCs of Building
MODEL RAILROAD CARS

WAYNE & MARY CAY WESOLOWSKI

TAB BOOKS Inc.
Blue Ridge Summit, PA

Notices

Elmer's is a trademark of Borden.
Kadee is a registered trademark of Kadee Quality Products Co.
Kodak is a registered trademark of Eastman Kodak.
Solvaset is a trademark and GOO is a registered trademark of Hobsco Inc.
X-acto is a registered trademark of Hunt/X-acto.

FIRST EDITION
SECOND PRINTING

Copyright © 1985 by TAB BOOKS Inc.
Printed in the United States of America

Library of Congress Cataloging in Publication Data

Wesolowski, Wayne E.
ABCs of building model railroad cars.

Includes index.
1. Railroads—Cars—Models. I. Wesolowski,
Mary Cay II. Title.
TF197.W365   1985   625.1'9   85-17325
ISBN 0-8306-1635-7 (pbk.)

TAB BOOKS Inc. offers software for
sale. For information and a catalog,
please contact TAB Software Department,
Blue Ridge Summit, PA 17294-0850.

Questions regarding the content of this book
should be addressed to:

Reader Inquiry Branch
TAB BOOKS Inc.
Blue Ridge Summit, PA 17294-0214

Contents

Foreword

MODELING RAILROAD FREIGHT CARS AND rolling stock presents an unending source of pleasure and an opportunity for creativity in the hobby. In fact, it is a rapidly growing part of model railroading, as the cars between the engine and the caboose receive increased attention from both individual modelers and manufacturers. There exists at present a wide range of kits, both simple-assembly and craftsman types, and an expanding number of ready-to-run models in relatively inexpensive plastic or limited-run brass forms. It would seem that there would be no need for serious rolling stock modeling; yet this is not the case.

Part of the reason for this need lies in the mixture of universal and unique elements that affect the nation's car fleet. Railroading moved out of its formative years about 125 years ago, after the American Civil War. While today's rolling stock certainly does not look like that of those days, the time-proven system of flanged wheel on steel rail remains. Car construction has been evolutionary—a continuum. Thus, a boxcar has remained a boxcar.

The basics of the design, and the required items to allow it to mix together with other freight cars in an international North American interchange pool, have not been discarded, nor will they be in the foreseeable future. One may not model, but can relate to, an older, or newer, boxcar.

Yet, all boxcars are not alike. So many things may be shipped in them that differences are inevitable, even at a specific point in history. They may be built in different ways, with different materials, and receive special fittings to protect their cargoes. Then, there are the variety of colors, heralds, and reporting marks that come from the number of railroads using them. The universal boxcar becomes rather special quite quickly.

What is true for boxcars, of course, is true for other types of cars. Take the century's production of freight and passenger cars, cut it in half, then choose the most common types. Commercial sources still could not supply every kind of car in every variation. Thus, there is a need for traditional and other methods of modelmaking.

A more important reason for the new strength of rolling stock modeling comes, I believe, from another source. We could look at statistics about the kinds of cars in service and how their numbers have changed over the years (the total is down to 1 and 1/2 million today, as compared to 2 million 20 years ago) and not come to an understanding of why a modeler would kitbash or scratchbuild yet another freight car. Studying car construction methods, and checking books on locomotives and car rosters are enjoyable, but not the cause of such interest. The main force behind the adding of details, the weathering, the kit bashing, and the scratchbuilding of rolling stock comes from one thing: a desire for excellence from within the individual modeler. The search for prototype fidelity, the experimenting and mastering of modeling techniques and materials, the hours spent researching car parts and the history of car construction—all of these grow out of that source.

I have known Wayne Wesolowski for many years, both as a collaborating author some time ago, and, more recently, as an editor. He is among the most creative modelers in the hobby today, and he has regularly devised new techniques and introduced new materials to those who have read his frequent articles, have attended one of his clinics at conventions, have read his previous book, or have seen his videotapes on building structures. He seeks excellence, achieves it, then helps others to do the same. I know that this latest sharing of information by Wayne will open new opportunities for those who open its covers.

William C. Schaumburg, Editor
Railroad Model Craftsman Magazine

Acknowledgments

MY DAD STARTED ME IN MODEL RAILROAD-ing when I was about 3 years old, sitting in a high chair while the trains ran all about me much to my delight. That was it . . . . I was hooked for life. Even when Mary Cay and I were engaged, we had many dates on locomotive fan trips all across Illinois. I'm sure her dad must have thought I was not very creative explaining our arrival home at 2 A.M. because "a locomotive axle bearing over-heated."

With that long a background in trains, it is very difficult, if not impossible, to thank all of those who had an influence on this book, but we do especially thank Edward and Dolores Wesolowski and Frances Debowski, our parents, who encouraged, cajoled, pushed, and finally said, "Forget the visits . . . just get that book done!" Through the years fellow modelers like Frank Pawlikowski, Paul Jones, John Kissinger, Lee Gustafson, Roger Witt, Tom Dyba, Larry Easton, Bob Pfister, Ted Hap-pel, Bill Stewart, Bill Lorence, and Dave Methlie (and Maggie) have shared their ideas and good times with us.

Two friends, Bob Walker and Al Westerfield, have taken the hobby one step further into commer-cial enterprises.

The editors of *Railroad Model Craftsman*, Tony Koester and Bill Schaumburg, have become good personal friends over the years, although they in-sisted that our writing improve with each submis-sion. Allen Keller and Russ Larson at *Model Railroader* and Kalmbach Video have introduced us to entirely new areas of model education com-munication.

Louis Koepel of the Quincy Mining Company, Tom Roberts, Paul Meier, and Al Henning all pro-vided a wealth of information about mining railroads and their facilities. We give an especially big thank you to Gail Hayes who types all our manuscripts from scribbled and patched rough drafts. Finally Mary Cay and I would like to acknowledge the many model railroaders who have offered advice, criticism, encouragement, and pleasure over our efforts.

Introduction

SEVERAL TIMES EACH DAY A CHICAGO AND Northwestern freight train lumbers through the small town of Marengo, Illinois (Fig. I-1). It hardly gets a turned head from most of the citizens, although you can see some children lined up for a chance to wave at the engineer. Frequently standing on his porch can be seen another observer, a bit older but just as intense. I'm that viewer and really quite unashamed to say that getting older has not diminished my fascination with trains. "Playing with trains" is fun at any age. We all need hobbies and forms of relaxation that will allow for a change from the daily routine and give some genuine feeling of accomplishment. Model railroading has grown as a hobby since the 1930s because it is multifaceted and allows the modeler to pick and choose from many areas of interest.

Some modelers like scenery, electronic controls, prototype operations, or sound effects. Others build cars, locomotives, and structures; any of these aspects can be pursued on various levels with different amounts of involvement (Figs. I-2 and I-3).

Perhaps one of the most enjoyable parts of model railroading, however, is building cars and rolling stock for your own pike (Figs. I-4 and I-5). Standing on my porch, which just happens to be a few hundred feet from the tracks, I can see a constant parade of locomotives and cars—new cars carrying freight to factories west of us; old cars in work trains to repair the rails. Cars, or more technically, *rolling stock*, are the backbone of railroading. In them are both the history and utility of this major transportation industry. I find it just truly fascinating to pick cars that I especially like and build them for my railroad empire (Fig. I-6).

How you go about collecting cars for your own railroad is a matter of personal preference. I have known modelers to purchase kits or ready-made equipment and collect literally hundreds of cars of all descriptions. They have the excellent collections of which anyone would be proud. Others wishing to be a little more personal about their models may take months to painstakingly build exact replicas of special cars—one of a kind, scratchbuilt

Fig. I-1. The Chicago and Northwestern Railroad serves the little town of Marengo, Illinois. Twice each day a freight lumbers through town to serve a foundry, a steel fabrication plant, several farm supply firms, and a few minor industries. On this cold winter day, the freight is switching the Farm Service store.

models—that no one else has. They, too, have a special brand of satisfaction.

Our purpose in this book is to take you through the world of railroad rolling stock. I feel there is a special satisfaction in saying "I built this model" that cannot be replaced with a ready-made model. The greater the degree of your involvement, the greater the satisfaction. Not every model I build is completely scratchbuilt, but the more I am a part of the process, the more fun it is.

We hope this little volume will give you a chance to look at different kinds of railroad cars, how the railroads actually built them, and how you might go about building models. We know that modelers have wide ranges of skills, and the person who programs computers all day, who lays stone, or who takes care of children might not want to scratchbuild an ornate private dining car from the 1880s. There is, however, a place for all of us

and we provide a sampling of suggestions that will help you now and some challenging ideas that will have you strive for more in the future. For those reasons this is really a beginner's book, but you decide what level of beginner. We look at model building from suggestions on how to get more out of the kits you buy, all the way to scratchbuilding old trolley cars.

You'll notice we made no mention of scale or gauge so far. That's because modeling really has little to do with the size models you finally construct, but rather with the skills you have and the materials you use. Therefore the book is divided into three parts by modeling material—wood, paper, and plastic. These are perhaps the most common modeling materials used in all scales. Metals probably should be in the group as well, but they take special skills that are beyond the beginning modeler. In each of these sections we treat the ma-

Fig. I-2. This elevated octagonal shanty was scratchbuilt entirely from pieces of styrene, following the prototype on the Milwaukee Road in LaCrosse, Wisconsin.

Fig. I-3. This large foundry follows the CB&Q prototype in Aurora, Illinois, and was built entirely from plaster castings that even included the windows. The model has that railroad "feeling" we are all trying to capture.

Fig. I-4. Dennis Storzak built this near-perfect model of a simple flat car, including every detail imaginable. The brakes actually work, and each board on the deck is individually scraped and weathered. To build this quality of a model, you must almost follow exact prototype construction procedures.

Fig. I-5. This cute little boom spraying car for a trolley line was built by Bob Brown, publisher of the *Narrow Gauge and Short Line Gazette*, over a single power truck. Many modelers buy the basic equipment for their pike in assembled form, then build up special cars like these (courtesy of Robert Brown).

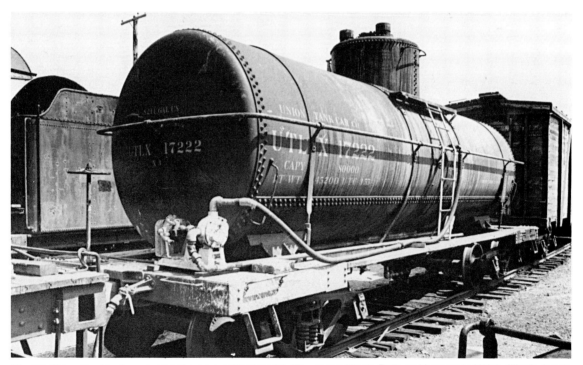

Fig. I-6. This retired tanker would make an excellent model. Now at the Illinois Railway Museum in Union, Illinois, it was last used to deliver oil to small tanks at rail sheds. The small pump on the deck was used to deliver oil at remote sites. The techniques described in this book will help you build such a model.

terial first, discussing its nature, uses, cutting and painting techniques, as well as suppliers. Also included are graded projects using that material, ranging from the very simple for neophytes to slightly more difficult projects. You pick the material and level at which to start.

No one is an expert at all these materials. We are just beginners at different levels. Some modelers have worked with wood for years, yet never tried plastic. Older moldelers probably have used paper, but not plastic. Newer kit manufacturers now routinely combine wood, metal, and plastic in kits because the new adhesives allow you to bond these materials with ease. There is a place for all of us.

Well, so much for the talking. The 4:15 is whistling for the grade crossing uptown and will soon be coming past. Come on out on the porch and watch her go by. I'll bet there are some interesting new cars you haven't seen before.

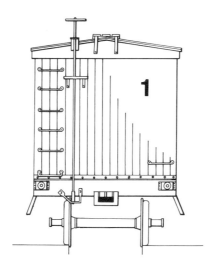

You and Your
Models— Some Basic Ideas

T O MAKE GOOD RAILROAD MODELS, YOU NEED not invest thousands of dollars in a full professional machine shop. What's needed are some rather simple tools and the desire to constantly improve your skills. Each model should be a little better, and as you learn new techniques improving your models should become second nature. There is no need to get fanatical, but the desire to "create" a special model really is what makes model building satisfying. With an easy kit, thousands of modelers have the same finished product, while with one that you've added some special details or actually scratchbuilt, you have the only one. Sound good? Read on.

RESEARCH AND STUDY

The library is a good place to get ideas for future projects. Old issues of the standard hobby magazines like *Model Railroader* and *Railroad Model Craftsman* are available at many large libraries. Browse through some of the more recent issues.

Study some of the modeling techniques and perhaps newer materials. Then look at some of the older, classic issues. Jack Work in the 1950s built beautiful cars from cardstock and a little stripwood. This was a period of rapid growth in scratchbuilding and the use of new and ever more precise building techniques—a kind of golden era. Even in the 1940s, however, credible models were made with common tools and a little imagination.

Of special value to the car builder are the cyclopedias now reprinted in whole or part by Newton Gregg in his Train Shed series (see the Appendix). These were the working manuals of actual railroad craftsmen who were building cars at that time. Manufacturers would take out ads heralding their new products and materials in the same books. Also journals like *Railway Age* and *Railway Age Gazette* were magazines of the railroad industry. Reading a few issues or volumes of these prototype journals will not only show you in great detail what was being built then but also give you a feeling for the ideas, dreams, and thoughts of the railroad men we often imagine ourselves to be. If you model the late 1920s like I do, these magazines can also be sources of information about cars, clothing styles, housing habits, and the like. Because several prototype journals are still published today, modelers from any era can use them for information. Check with the engineering section of a large public or university library. Old retail catalogs like Sears and Roebuck can also be a source of information about the many small details that make a great modeling scene.

Many of the old journals and the cyclopedias contain large numbers of scale drawings rather than pictures of cars and rolling stock, which are a real boon to model builders. More about drawings later.

Besides the major modeling magazines, a number of smaller, but highly specialized, publications have appeared lately, including the *Narrow Gauge and Short Line Gazette* for mining and lumber railroad fans and *Mainline Modeler* for the dedicated modeler of more contemporary prototypes. If you have an interest in a particular railroad, check if a historical society for that specific road exists. A number of these groups are listed in the Appendix. Typically staffed by modelers like yourself, these groups, usually with great enthusiasm, try to preserve the history and personality of a particular railroad or group of railroads. Many publish their own newsletters with information simply not available anywhere else. The quality ranges from first-class publications on coated paper to ditto newsletters, but if you love the "Fog Bottom and Over the Hill RR," sharing information with others about your special interest may overshadow the lack of a professionally edited journal. When you are writing to these kinds of organizations, it's best to enclose a self-addressed, stamped envelope to speed an answer to you. The pressure of family, church, job, and editing a newsletter may slow down a reply. Also be specific with your questions if possible. "Send me everything you have on every class of boxcars on the Pennsylvania RR" may not get a reply.

Catalogs from the major suppliers, such as W.K. Walthers, are now more like mini-modeling manuals with valuable hints on construction techniques.

The latest entry into the model education field is home videotapes, such as the scenery and wood construction tapes by Kalmbach Publishing Company. They may not be *Star Wars*, but to a railroad modeler they may be better.

Membership in the National Model Railroad Association (NMRA) may also be helpful in looking for information. Besides receiving a first-quality monthly magazine, membership includes the right to attend divisional (local), regional, and national meetings of the group. At these meets modelers come together to hear talks by experts in the modeling field, share ideas about projects, visit railroad facilities, and generally share the fellowship of a common interest in trains and models. One of the highlights is frequently the model contest, where entries in various catagories are judged in areas of basic construction. (Fig. 1-1) I spend a lot of time in the contest room looking at the structures and rolling stock. You can get many new ideas by talking with the judges and entrants. When you feel ready, enter a contest yourself. Many regions have separate contests for kit and scratchbuilt models. Ask the judges for constructive criticism and build your skills.

For me, though, the best part of the meeting is to see old friends and find new ones with a common interest. It can be just marvelous, relaxing enjoyment (Figs. 1-2 and 1-3).

THE WORK AREA

In building railroad models, my actual work areas have ranged from a little desk in the corner of the bedroom to the major part of the attic which I now use. Although my wife refers to the modeling area as the octopus since it constantly is grabbing more storage and display room, the actual building process uses only a few square feet of space. As the project continues, this area begins to fill with scrap wood, paper cutoffs, paint bottles, rejected parts, etc. At some point a general clean-up is declared, the area is cleaned, and the work continues. So the

Fig. 1-1. Bob Brown, publisher of the *Narrow Gauge and Short Line Gazette,* built this beautiful stream shovel primarily from styrene and special metal castings that he made from his own patterns. His work was rewarded by a first place in the Maintenance of Way category at the 1971 National Model Railroad Association's national meeting.

Fig. 1-2. Charlie Dyxin is the contest chairman for the Midwest Region of the National Model Railroad Association. A meticulous craftsman, extreme detail has always been a sign of his work. One of Charlie's favorites is this large-scale model (1/2″ = 1′0″) freelanced model of a wood caboose. The level of detail is really fascinating, including a full brake system.

Fig. 1-3. The caboose roof lifts off to reveal a complete interior, including a plug in the sink drain and coal in the bucket next to the stove. The small cabinet doors open, but I didn't smell any coffee brewing. Come on, Charlie, you can do better!!

first requirement is only a small area set aside for your work (Fig. 1-4).

Next, and perhaps most important, is the lighting. To build a good model, you have to see it very clearly. There should be no shadows or hidden corners. If a model is built in very strong light, it will appear even better in normal light. I use two lamps on flexible shafts mounted directly above my work area at about a 45-degree angle to the modeling surface. Shadows will hide details, but more importantly they will hide glue spots, gaps, and small imperfections that may look like chasms and huge blobs when brought out into the layout lighting. Another factor to consider is the type of lighting used. Your model should be built under the same form of lighting in which it will be displayed. Fluorescent lighting tends to bring out the blues and greens, while incandescent emphasizes the oranges and reds. Models built under one type of lighting

may look very strange if placed on a layout with a different kind of lighting. Even normal sunlight is different than most artificial lighting.

Next you need some kind of cutting surface. I suggest a small piece of pressed wood or fiberboard that has absolutely no grain. You can also use glass. Don't use a piece of wood with a grain, no matter how smooth the surface may be. When your knife or cutting tool breaks through the work piece, it may begin to follow the grain in the wood and pull away from your straightedge, giving a wavy cut for what seems like no reason at all. Using a grainless cutting base will minimize this problem.

USING THE CAMERA

Surprisingly, another good tool for model building is the camera. Nothing is a more stern judge of your work than an enlarged picture of the finished model. Every seam, glue spot, and error just seems to jump out at you. Also the camera is your number-one tool for capturing the prototype in making new models. A visit to your local railroad museum with a good camera can bring home an entire winter's worth of new car-building projects. For the beginner it might be easier to work from photos in magazines or books rather than try a complete scratchbuilding project now. If a car catches your fancy, though, I suggest getting many photos and a few dimensions today. Tomorrow it may be off to Patagonia, Arizona or a bad order track, and there is no way to replace those pictures not taken.

Fig. 1-4. Son Steven sits in the small swivel chair in front of his dad's bench. Well, it's actually an old kitchen cabinet organizer. Notice the two flexible shaft lamps that help eliminate shadows. Several shelves to the right hold small parts and paint. Small tools are in the rack just in front of Steven. Of course, absolute neatness is not required. Frankly I clean the bench only when things get so cluttered I can't find the model of interest. An interesting feature of my workshop is that the switch which turns off the lights also controls several of the room sockets. When I leave at the end of a work session and turn off the lights, any of the smaller tools are also disconnected, therefore I never worry about leaving a small soldering iron plugged in overnight. In addition, a radio goes on and off with that same switch; so the radio playing indictes that the power is on.

Some of my models are built from photographs my dad took with a simple Kodak Brownie box camera. For its time, it was a fine family camera. Today I would suggest purchasing a simple SLR (single lens reflex) 35mm camera. They are light, portable, and reasonably priced and can easily double for family and vacation photographs. For a car project, I will take perhaps 100 black and white photographs around, under, and over the car. This may sound like a horrendously expensive extravagance, but it really isn't. First, the film comes in 36-exposure rolls, and I could have the processor only develop and make a contact sheet. The small negatives are placed on one sheet of photographic paper and a print made of all of them at one time. You get 36 tiny prints on an 8- x -10 piece of paper. These can then be studied with a magnifying glass if necessary, and only those of the most interest are printed in a larger size. The small contact sheets also simplify storage and filing of the photographs if you are not going to start the project at once (Fig. 1-5).

My main camera is an old model I bought used 15 years ago for about half the new price, yet it has served me well all these years. Actually most of my photographic equipment was purchased used because many of the items are very well-made and the amateur photographer just doesn't work them that much. Of course with the purchase of any used item, it's best to deal with a reputable sales firm that will back up your purchase should something go wrong.

The finished prints will give you a chance to study, in detail, but at a relaxed pace, the car you would like to build. I like to take a stack of prints, turn on the ball game, and just dream a little about how I plan to build the model. How will these pieces go together? Where does that rod go? Why are the ends shaped this way? You actually learn a lot about construction when you model rolling stock.

For those with photography as a second hobby or with a photographer friend, the cost of photographs can be brought down to a few dollars by developing, enlarging, and printing them yourself.

For all my work I use Kodak plus X (ASA 125)

black-and-white film which I develop and print myself, but any camera shop will develop and make the contact sheet at a nominal cost. If you want to try a little photography yourself without making a major investment, many high schools and junior colleges have photography classes where your car project could become your assignment. Also larger cities have rental photo darkrooms where you may use equipment, chemicals, and photographic papers for an hourly fee.

A few color slides will give you the basis for painting and weathering your model. Also the slides can be used to make rough drawings of the car by taping a piece of paper to a wall, then moving the slide projector back and forth until the image of the car is square on the wall and enlarged to an appropriate size. Finally the car can be traced directly on the paper—voila, instant plans. Most important is to get the pictures today! Tomorrow is too late because cars are moved and never seen again.

GENERAL HINTS

A few more general thoughts that I will enlarge upon later in the text follow. In the vast majority of models I build, all the parts are prestained or painted, especially if the trim or smaller pieces are of a contrasting color. Once the model has been assembled, it's almost impossible to do a neat job of painting the trim without running over into the rest of the model. Painting is probably done best with a spray can or airbrush painting tool. Brushing is okay if you want the model to look old or don't need a very smooth finish, but a new smooth model almost always needs a sprayed finish.

When applying adhesives of almost any kind, keep the joints very tight and firmly held with a clamp or weight until the glue has a chance to set. The time may range from seconds for the super glues to 24 hours for some epoxies. Just a little glue, good contact between the surfaces, and a full setting time are the three basics of gluing.

If you plan to make several copies of the same part or section of a car, use a jig, or more correctly, a *fixture*. These are guides or small tabs glued to a base and used to position the various parts in place exactly the same way for each replication (Fig. 1-6).

Fig. 1-5. Collected on one sheet are the direct prints of a full roll of 35mm film. This "contact sheet" provides a simple and easy way to inspect and store pictures.

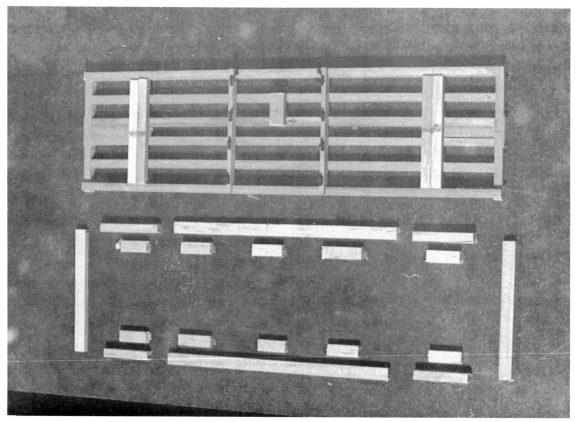

Fig. 1-6. If more than three or four of an item are needed, I like to use a fixture; that is, some kind of device to hold pieces exactly in place while the adhesive sets. In this case the car frame on the top fits exactly into the holder, or fixture, at the bottom. This fixture, made for me by Bill Schaumburg, ensures that each car is exactly the same length and width. Additional spacer blocks are used to position the other pieces of wood that make up the frame.

Fixtures make it easy to keep parts aligned and exactly positioned while other components are added. Although it is only a personal rule of thumb, I tend to use a fixture if I need to make three copies or more of a section of a car.

Don't worry about going stale on a project. I can't remember a single project that I started on a Friday and had finished on the layout on Monday morning. Interest ebbs and flows; so I like to actually have three to five projects going at the same time with a few in the thinking stage. My work room is by no means organized. Some projects take weeks and others longer—I had one coaling tower that took 10 years to complete. Setbacks (including dropping a toolbox on it) and new sources of information kept me rebuilding, quitting, and

rebuilding again for over a decade. The model, though, may be one of my best.

To keep all of these projects from getting totally confused with each other, I use metal trays from an old store display (cafeteria trays would work as well) to keep the plans, parts, special tools, and miscellaneous stuff together for each project. When my interest wanes, the whole project is packed up in its tray and put on a shelf until I feel like going at it again. Those trays have saved me a lot of frustration and have kept several projects from dying.

One last piece of advice: details, details, details. The one feature that usually separates an ordinary kit or even scratchbuilt car from the really first-class one is details. An extra vent, little nuts and bolts, castings, grab irons, ornate observation railings, and a little simulated stained glass in a passenger car all add that little extra touch that makes your cars special. You need not try to make these detail pieces by yourself because there are literally thousands of castings and parts available from a wide variety of manufacturers. They are cast in metal for crisp detail or less expensively in plastic. You can purchase anything from brake cylinders to tiny signs saying "Passengers are requested not to spit on the platform." With the new rapid-setting super glues like "Hotstuff," it is no problem to mix metal, plastic, and wood all in the same model and still have excellent results. Watching visitors ooh and aah over a model as they discover more details can be very satisfying.

COMPONENT PARTS

For years I had the notion that literally everything on a model had to be scratchbuilt to make it worthwhile. As I grew older and wiser, I realized that sort of thinking may be true for contest models but not for models built for fun. We are very fortunate that a number of manufacturers have produced literally thousands of component parts in every scale for building our cars and structures. Rather than building each and every piece of a model, you can purchase brake equipment, railings, end castings, couplers, steps, seats, doors, windows, roof vents, brake wheels, and so on. There is no reason why you should not be able to build a car from scratch or highly detail a kit with these parts. Don't be afraid, either, to mix manufacturers and even scales. An HO diesel hatch may make a perfect O-scale clean-out door, or an N-scale wagon wheel may be the perfect HO pipe valve wheel.

These parts come in metal and plastic and range in price from rather expensive to pennies each. Look for parts that are crisp with little flash (thin material pushed out between the die halves) and that show details clearly.

A suggestion, though—if you see a part you like, especially from a small manufacturer, buy it today and maybe get a few extra for the future. Many of these companies are small hobbyist operations, and the press of family and primary occupation make most of them short-lived enterprises. A good collection of parts safely in your drawer is much better than saying "I wish I had bought more when they were available." Take detailing of kits and scratchbuilt models as far as you are comfortable, but most of all have fun. That's the whole idea of model railroading: Let's move on now to some basic suggestions about where to begin.

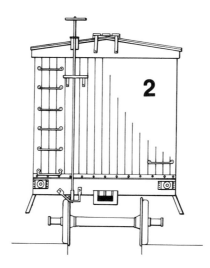

Where to Begin!

ERHAPS ONE OF THE FIRST QUESTIONS THAT comes to mind is "Where do I begin?" The strongest force in the world is not gravity or nuclear attractions but the simple inertia of having to start a new project or delve into a new area. It's been that way for years with me. I hesitated to work with plastics for more than 10 years, only to find when I got started that I really loved the material. The same inertia, or resistance to something new, may be your problem as well.

As a prod to get things going, I suggest browsing through a good, comprehensive hobby catalog like one from Walther's Hobby Shop (See the Appendix) or looking through the advertisements in several back issues of *Railroad Model Craftsman* or *Model Railroader*. Find a good kit that captures your fancy. There are several varieties of kits, beginning at what is called the *shake together* type where there is really little construction, just gluing or screwing together the major components to make the finished model. These kits certainly have their place in the hobby—to give the absolute begin-

ner a little fun and to allow anyone to quickly build up a large collection of rolling stock.

We're looking for something a little more challenging, however, sometimes called *craftsmen kits*. Now you don't have to have a Master Model Railroader's certificate to build one of these—just a little experience at building some of the easier kits and the general tools described in later sections, plus the desire to build ever better models.

Your local hobby shop is another great place to check out some of these kits. Try to stop in at a time when things are not too rushed and talk with the owner or permanent sales staff. They are generally friendly and a fountain of information on model building. Although much of their business is focused on selling finished models, they are generally experienced modelers on their own and have lots of experience to share with you. By knowing you and your skill level, a good dealer can point to just the right kit or type of kit to keep the challenge alive without overextending your abilities. The craftsman kit usually has a lot of little bags of parts, plenty of uncut wood (frequently color coded), and good instruction sheets. The best kits are very near to scratchbuilding a car, with the exception of the step-by-step assembly sequence.

Sometimes, however, all is not so rosy. Some modelers have real problems with these kits and go back to the box shakers. Why? I suppose there are a lot of reasons, but I would guess one of them is the little frustrations that begin to add up and finally if everything doesn't look perfect, they just quit. Since I like to scratchbuild, I sometimes just get tired of following someone else's instructions and either finish it off as I would like to do it or just give up. There are a number of unfinished kits on my shelves waiting for that quiet day when I have time. To help you complete the first craftsman kit or any kit, I thought it would be useful to take you through a kit I'm building as I build it—good and bad, goof and all. As I write this, I have not even started, so this one may wind up in the dumpster as well. Read on as the saga unfolds. I'll keep a little diary and pictures so we can follow the progress.

DAY 1

My passenger car collection is rather weak since I really like freight cars; so I thought a kit of a nice combine (half coach, half baggage car) would be a good addition to the roster. I searched through my unbuilt kit collection and chose a LaBelle Woodworking 1906 Milwaukee Road combine kit. I had plenty to choose from since O scalers are incredible pack rats—not that many O scalers have layouts since the scale demands large, large rooms, but they do seem to buy a lot of kits and put them on shelves.

It seems to me the average life of an O-scale manufacturer is about 2 years. You see a big splash of ads, some great-looking kits, and then the enthusiasm begins to die. Perhaps this is because many of the smaller specialty manufacturers are basement operations, and the pressures of job, family, and community become too much along with the ordering, shipping, backordering, collecting, corresponding, etc. In any case, my advice for everyone is if you see a good kit from a small

manufacturer buy it now, maybe buy two. Tomorrow the kit and the supplier may be gone. This would also apply to the limited editions from the major suppliers, since many of those kits are hard to get the minute they are released.

Back to the journal. While watching my favorite professional football team get pommeled again, I opened the box, removed the plans, and did a little dreaming. I could see a pullman green combine, (just a little dirty) pulling into my Morgan's Bluff depot behind a husky consolidation, with a couple of freight cars to make up the daily mixed train. Looked good . . . . this was going to be a fun project. Then I got down to business.

Read the directions at least once. Get a feel for what you have to do. I read them once, then twice. Whew! There is a lot to do. I'm kind of confused since the instructions apply to four different types of cars all based on the same fundamental kit, but with slight to major variations. I'd better go at this slowly (Fig. 2-1).

DAY 2

The plans are nice and big, but as with so many manufacturers, to save money they printed the instructions and some of the drawings on one side and more of the drawings on the back. This means in the middle of the project when you've covered the bench with parts, glue, tools etc., you will have to dig out the plans, flip them over for a look at drawing "J," then turn them back over to keep going. Off I went to the photocopying machine to make a copy of everything. This is also helpful when you spill the paint on view "A" and can't clean it off. Careful, though, as some photocopiers will not copy exactly but introduce a 3 to 5 percent error. Check your plans with a scale rule. Measure one of the longer dimensions, like the full length of the car.

DAY 3

One of the things I like to do most with a kit is sift through the little packets of metal and plastic castings that accompany the wooden parts. These are the little gems that will highlight the finished model. I usually read through the plans and direc-

Fig. 2-1. There's a lot to the kit I have to assemble. I'm confused with the drawings, and it will be a real challenge to make the mountain of parts into a finished car.

tions to get an idea of how parts are to go together and what castings are needed. Tonight I came home after a long day of especially disheartening meetings and thought the casting preparation would be just what I needed to cheer me up.

First the parts have to be trimmed and filed to remove signs of the casting process, which usually includes flash or small thin films of metal that oozed between the mold pieces as the liquid solidified. Casting imperfections usually are at the parting line where the mold parts separate. Look at a casting of a brake cylinder. The reservoir should be a perfectly round cylinder. Almost all castings will show a clear line or offset where the mold was joined. This is not unusual, nor does it mean the part is of low quality. Of course the better the casting, the fewer corrections you should have to make.

For the flash I use a sharp X-acto knife to slice away the excess metal. A small set of pattern or jeweler's files may be used to finish any pieces too large for the knife to cut.

The castings may also require the use of files to remove imperfections. I find it advantageous to use a larger file, but with a fine cutting surface (not a coarse cut like a bastard file). Using a file too small for the job leaves a series of ruts, rather than a smooth surface. For curved surfaces, round files are a must. The soft metals used for model castings will quickly fill the file with metal cuttings. I clean these out with a stiff wire brush and draw the file across a piece of chalk to fill and protect the grooves.

Painting comes next. Paint will not properly adhere to a dirty or greasy surface; so the parts should be first washed with a toothbrush and a liquid soap, then rinsed with lots of water, and finally rinsed with alcohol to produce rapid drying. Once the washing is done, it's best to try and handle the parts as little as possible because finger oils will act as a barrier to the paint. Some modelers will add a soaking in vinegar to act as a mild etching agent to give the surface a little tooth, or roughness, to better hold the paint. I have not found that necessary.

Once the parts are dry, I like to hold them either in clothespins or hemostatlike clamps while either brush painting or spraying them, especially more complicated parts. There really is no substitute for the beautifully smooth surface that can be achieved with an airbrush (Fig. 2-2). I have terrible sinus problems so I use Polly S water-based paints from Flouquil. If I were able to do it, I would have the first coat of all my models be a lacquer-based modeling paint which is allowed to thoroughly dry for several days at a minimum. Boy,

I know this is hard, but if your castings seem to easily scratch or chip, it's because the paint has set but not really hardened. All the parts received a base coat of grimy black. Of course the area being held in the clamps or clothespin cannot be painted. With a little patience, you can wait a few minutes until the paint sets then remove the clamp and touch up the raw area. Finally the part is placed on the bench in such a way to keep wet areas from sticking.

Once the grimy black has set, a little Polly S "rust" thinned with plenty of water is dabbed on here and there. The black castings are just too uniform, and the rust serves to highlight the part. When this has dried, a final dab of Polly S boxcar red with the brush dipped in a little isopropyl (rubbing) alcohol is scattered about. The paint is not truly soluble in the alcohol and the mixtures tend to puddle and precipitate, leaving scaly rust chips.

Notice the use of three types of paint. The lac-

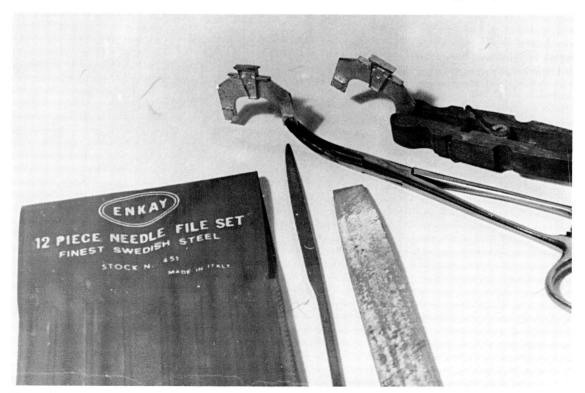

Fig. 2-2. Several files were used to clean parts, which can be held in a small clamp called a hemostat. The airbrush will give a fine, smooth finish to the paint job.

quer base is not affected by the water-solvent Polly S, which in turn is coated with a quick-setting alcohol mix. Careful! Too much rubbing with the alcohol coating may start to dissolve the others. Use just a blotch and dab here and there. I learned about this method of using different kinds of paints in layers from Art Curren of *Model Railroader* magazine at a clinic he gave at the Rock Valley Division of the National Model Railroad Association.

DAY 4

Now the car really starts to come together. This perhaps is the most exciting time of building a kit. There is a rule in business called the 20/80 principle. Seems like 20 percent of the staff does 80 percent of the work, or 20 percent of your bills account for 80 percent of the debt, and so on. I feel that something like the first 20 percent of your kit construction time represents 80 percent of the results. You start with just a box of parts and instructions and in a relatively short time the walls go together; the coverings go on; the doors and windows are in place. This is the real thrill of construction. The rest is detailing—adding handrails, window trim, roofing.

You really must be careful that the last 80 percent doesn't tire you out and let the project die. I try to look at each little project as a new beginning so I can take advantage of the 20 percent enthusiasm all over again. If all else fails, try putting the project aside, but not away, and start again on another day.

I never cease to be amazed at the variety of new products constantly being introduced into the model railroad field. Sometimes, too, I fail to take advantage of new materials while feeling comfortable sticking with old ones. This kit is a good example. Although I've been building wood models for more than 20 years, I had always used a white or water-based glue for joining large pieces (over 1/2 inch), with the same problem: warping. The solution was to hold a joint firmly in place with huge weights until dry. Even then the warping was noticeable.

With this car kit, I had the same problem. A little light went on. I had purchased at a discount-liquidator's store a couple of tubes of Testor's cement for Wood Models at a ridiculously low price like 5¢ per tube (final closeout). Anyway this seemed like a good place to try it out. Each piece of wood was coated with the cement and allowed to slightly harden, then the pieces were joined and allowed to set. This adhesive worked beautifully, giving tight, strong joints with no warping. I would recommend it for gluing any large-surface wood project like scribed wood on the side of a car (Fig. 2-3).

Well, enough of the warm-ups. It was time to jump in and start working on the model. The project began with two long wooden sides already cut out for doors and windows. I used a small file and a bit of sandpaper to clean up any fuzz around the opening. Next step was to glue on pieces 2, 3, and 4 as window posts. I couldn't find them! There are 16 windows; so there should be a bunch of posts someplace.

About 20 minutes of searching convinced me that I had a defective kit—Yuck! Finally I noticed several pieces of sheetwood had a cutout on the back that would allow them to fit into the window slots. I reread the instructions . . . "separate and glue on" . . . These were the posts with extra detail, but they came in blocks of four that had to be cut apart. Also I discovered that for my kit—the combine—only part #2 was needed. Part #3, at least at this point, only was used on other versions of the kits. I'm still not too sure about #4 yet. Anyway these pieces were cut apart, and using only a tiny bit of glue were attached to both precut sides. The sides were finished in short order.

DAY 5

Well, I'm lying. It's not Day 5 but about 3 months later. Guess I either lost interest or was a little afraid to put the sides and ends together and see what I had made. When I did get the courage to glue those ends on, the car didn't look too bad. I made sure to assemble it on a good, flat surface to make sure everything fit tightly along the bottom. I could correct things along the top when the roof was added.

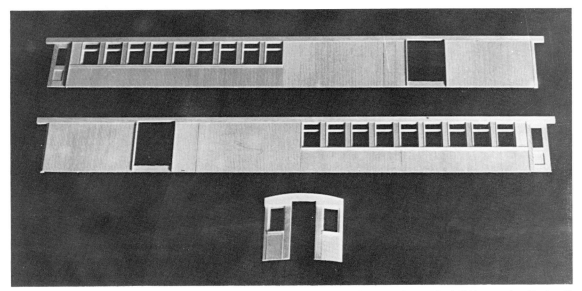

Fig. 2-3. Using a solvent-based wood cement, the sides went together without much trouble. I did have a few "bulges" where the sides began to pull away. I squirted a little glue under these spots and used plenty of weights to hold the piece flat while the glue completely set.

Fig. 2-4. The body is assembled, but required a putty to fill several joints that didn't fit well. The roof comes from the manufacturer correctly contoured, but is square at the ends. Both the roof and the top ends of the car must be carved and sanded to shape.

DAY 6

While the body sets up (I've added the sides now), the next big challenge is the roof. The kitmaker has provided a beautifully contoured roof (Fig. 2-4), but the ends have to be cut down to a rounded shape. Now the "experts" tell us to "carve and finish the roof ends with a knife and sandpaper." I've tried this in the past and after hours of careful carving and sanding I'd removed 1/8 inch with 3/4 inch to go. There may be those of you out there who like hours of carving and sanding. I waited for a sale at Sears and bought a belt sander (Fig. 2-5). Although it is not a normal modeling tool, it's great for removing large amounts of material in a hurry, and you can use it to sharpen kitchen knives! Shaping the roof took only 15 minutes. Now for painting. The car was done in coach green—a kind of olive drab—with an airbrush. I was really pleased

Fig. 2-5. A large belt sander is used to finish the car roof. Although the machine is bigger than most modelers need, it certainly removes the frustration when you have a lot of material to remove.

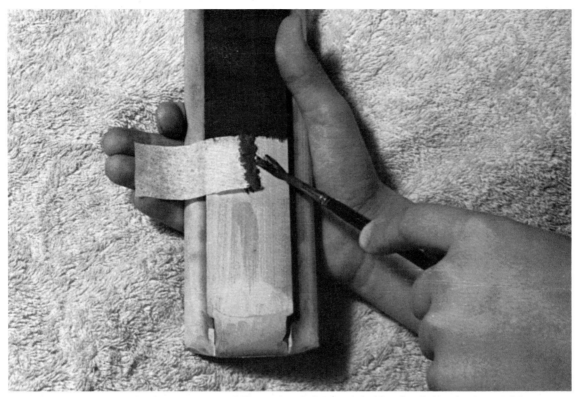

Fig. 2-6. Tissue is used to simulate a canvas roof. The surface is first coated with painted, then the tissue is laid in place.

Fig. 2-7. The completed combine, except for lettering and trucks. The tissue-covered roof has a very convincing texture.

with the coverage and texture. The car did have a few gaps, and even a hole here and there. These were filled with Squadron Green putty, a fast-drying filler used by model airplane buffs. It dries with little shrinkage and can be easily sanded.

The roof should look like one with an old canvas cover; it needs just a bit of texture. To simulate this, I used ordinary bathroom tissue. Kitchen paper toweling could also be used (Fig. 2-6). First you must separate the tissue down to just one ply. Cut each ply into about 3 scale-foot-wide strips. Next cover a small section of roof with a heavy coat of grimy black. While the paint is still wet, position a strip of the tissue in the wet paint. Use a brush dampened with solvent to set the tissue completely in the paint. Add more paint if needed, but try not to add so much that you hide the paper texture. While the roof was drying, I added all the metal castings under the car.

One other point: for some reason the manufacturer instructs you to put on the baggage doors long after the rest of the car is finished. I dutifully followed the instructions and then had to paint the doors separately after they had been put on the car. Of course I had put all the airbrushing equipment away; so I grabbed a brush and just kind of splashed on the paint. Remember the problem of warping with too much water-based glue? The same is true of too much solvent. My baggage doors puckered into two roller coaster doors. To save the project, I quickly put some paint on the inside of the door. This causes puckering in both directions and reduces warping. Then the door was clamped between two pieces of wood and allowed to dry. I made a mental note to photograph only the better side.

My car is almost done (Fig. 2-7), but before we go to Day 7 we're going to take a break—rather like the *Perils of Pauline* or the afternoon soaps—and go on to other projects. Will Wayne finish the combine? Will he give up? Will Mary Cay mistake the combine for fireplace kindling? To find out the answer tune into Chapter 13, where we will learn about adding decals and final weathering.

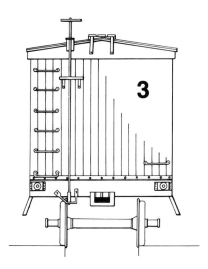

Basic Tools

T O MAKE GOOD RAILROAD MODELS YOU DON'T need to invest thousands of dollars in a professional machine shop. Modeling is relatively inexpensive and can be successfully started with a minimum of tools. A list of tools which I feel is a starting point can be found in Table 3-1. My collection has grown in more than 20 years of scratchbuilding through sale purchases, trading, scrounging, and modifying.

MEASURING AND MARKING TOOLS

Your most effective weapons in creating accurate models are the various measuring devices. Although they come in a variety of forms, all rulers are designed to make a comparison between a known dimension and another item. Therefore, your first investment in the line of tools should be the very best *scale rule* you can afford. Usually this would be a metal rule engraved with scale corresponding to the regular model scales—usually HO, O, S, and possibly N. It reads directly in scale feet and inches and is your prime source of ac-

curacy. Be sure that the ruler you are contemplating purchasing has clear and sharp markings that are not likely to wear off. It may also have additional scales (possibly full-size metric or English measurements) on the reverse side. Precise measurements are essential, and since your ruler is your primary method of measuring, and therefore, building your models, it really must be good.

For more exacting work, a *scale caliper* is very useful (Fig. 3-1). Although they are relatively expensive, if you need to know a dimension down to a scale bee's wingspan, the caliper is your tool. It's a precision measuring tool engraved with scale feet and inches and is read to the nearest 1/8 scale inch. You can really determine if a 2 × 4 really is 2 × 4. I also use the caliper to transfer dimensions directly to the work. It can be used to check spacing and will function as a depth gauge. The exact dimensions can be easily set on the caliper and then the work fashioned to fit the dimension.

A good *machinist's ruler* reading in 1/64 or, bet-

Table 3-1. Suggested Starter's Set of Basic Tools.

2 X-acto Knife Handles
1 Package each #11, #16 X-acto Knife Blades
1 Zona Saw—Fine Tooth
1 Scale Rule—12″ Length
1 Set Small Drills or Selected Common Sizes
1 Pin Vise for Drills
1 Package Single-Edged Razor Blades
1 Miter Box
1 Pair Tweezers
1 Set Pattern Files
1 Large File (Mill Face) 6″ or longer
  Assorted Small Pieces Flex-i-Grit and Sandpaper
1 Large Bag Spring-Type Clothespins
  Weights
  Number 4H Pencils
1 Scriber (Pin Struck in Wood Dowel)
1 Square (Inexpensive Combination Type)
1 Small Vise

ter yet, 1/100 inch (Fig. 3-2) would be helpful, too. It would be most useful for a modeler in a scale that relates directly to the English units (O: 1/4 inch = 1 foot and S: 3/16 inch = 1 foot). A finely divided metric rule would be better for the metric scales (HO: 3.5mm = 1 foot and N: 1.9mm = 1 foot). Thinking in scale feet and inches exclusively takes away the hassle and confusion of making numerous scale conversions.

A long steel *straightedge* is terrific for scribing lines, and a short one for easy handling in cramped spaces. Plastic or wooden rulers can be cut by knives. Always cut with a ruler in place because a handheld cut simply will not be straight. Also use the straightedge to cover the material you want to protect, so if the knife slips it will cut the scrap piece and not the good one. This may take a little juggling and turning of the pieces, but it is still a good habit to get into.

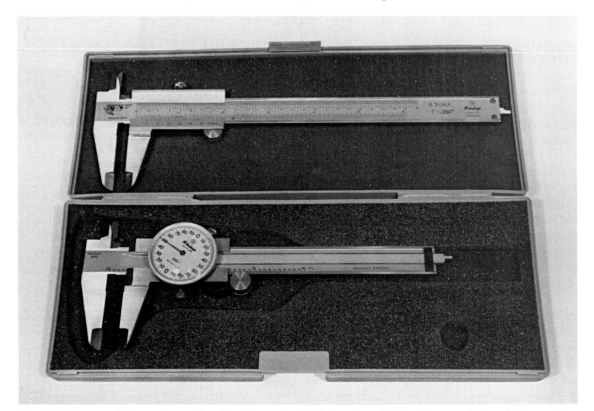

Fig. 3-1. At the top of the case is a scale caliper that reads to 1/8 of an O-scale inch. For very crical modeling, a caliper is the ultimate tool. The lower caliper has a dial reading in 0.001″ directly.

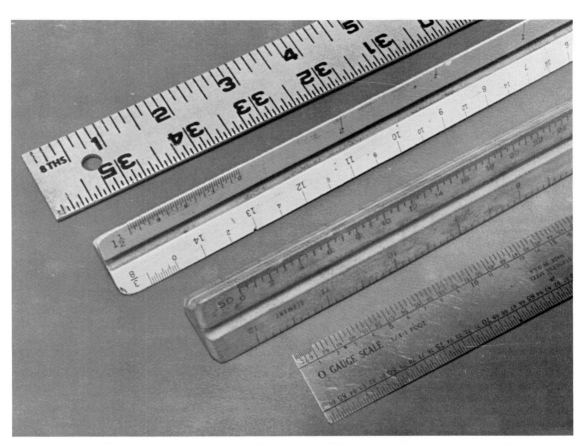

Fig. 3-2. Several different types of rulers are used by modelers. At the top is a simple yardstick used for very crude measurements. The second is a triangular architect's rule with six different scale rules in one. Because it is made from wood or plastic, it cannot be employed for a straightedge when cutting. Its major use is for reading or making plans in different scales. The third ruler is an engineer's scale with six different numerical scales, also used for reading drawings. The bottom metal ruler is a model railroad scale rule. Scales include O, HO, and S, plus metric and ordinary English scales on the reverse side. This is the real workhorse of a modeler's collection and should be of the best quality possible.

Dividers are two-legged instruments used to transfer dimensions from the plan to the work piece. If you have drawings printed in your scale, you can transfer the dimensions directly without the use of a scale rule. With their very sharp points, the dividers can be used to make small holes for reference points on the work piece.

Not all pencils, no matter how finely sharpened, are appropriate for use in modeling work. Pencils will dull quickly with use if they are sharpened to a point. A dot made with a dull pencil will be several scale inches in diameter. If used, *pencils* should be quite hard (4H) and sharpened to a chisel point on a piece of sandpaper (Fig. 3-3).

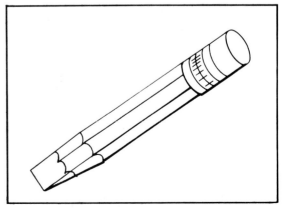

Fig. 3-3. A pencil with a chisel point.

A *scriber* gives a sharper and more consistent line than a pencil. One can be made inexpensively by grinding off the head of a straight pin and forcing it into a dowel for a handle (Fig. 3-4).

Since many lines must be drawn exactly square to the edge of a piece of material, you'll need a *square* of some sort. A 6-inch combination square I got at Sears is a good place to start. I also use a fine 3-inch machinist's square for working with smaller pieces.

CUTTING TOOLS

For cutting I use a *hobby knife* with exchangeable blades. Much of my work is done with X-acto #16 and #11 blades. The #16 blades are for rough cuts, and the #11s for getting into corners and very crisp cuts. Here's a tip: you will want the sharpest knife possible for cutting tiny pieces of trim or making a very crisp cutout. I put a piece of tape on the handle with the sharpest blade. As soon as the blade begins to dull, I transfer it to a second handle for making rough cuts. This way you always know which will give that crisp, sharp slicing action.

Use several light cuts, rather than trying to bear down and cut the piece of wood in a slice or two. For a piece of wood 1/16 inch thick, 8 to 10 strokes would be about right. For cutting out windows and interior pieces, I first mark the opening with a pencil filed to a chisel-shaped point, which holds its very sharp edge longer. Then with a very sharp, small drill, I make a hole in each corner of the opening. Using the metal straightedge to protect the good pieces, I then cut out the opening, starting and stopping at the small holes, which keep you from running on past the ends of the opening. A small, square file will sharpen any rounded corners.

Since knife blades are rather inexpensive, I frequently grind them to different shapes for special cutting jobs. The knife blade in Fig. 3-5 is made from a #16 blade and is shaped to score scribed siding to simulate the ends of boards without cutting into the adjoining pieces.

You'll also need a *backsaw* or razor saw for cutting thicker pieces. Usually a *miter box* is used to hold the wood pieces in place. I built a longer-than-normal miter box for trestle and extra-long wood pieces. With any miter box, the saw guides will begin to wear after a while, and the saw will wobble in the groove. Of course this gives a poor cut, but the groove can easily be renewed by using an ordinary square and cutting a new groove right in your miter box.

Single-edged razor blades are another good modeling tool. Although they cannot get into tight corners, they are inexpensive and will slice right through most wood, plastic, and paper. Both razors and knife blades dull quickly, so replace them often. It would not be unusual to use 5 to 10 blades constructing a complex car. All of these blades can be purchased in 100-piece bulk packs at reasonable

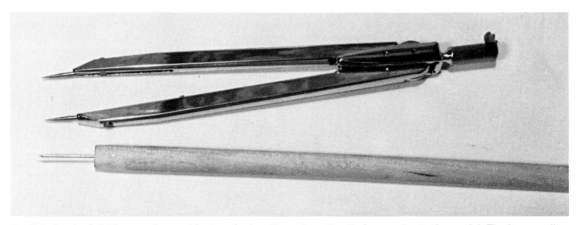

Fig. 3-4. A pair of dividers can be used for transferring dimensions directly from a plan to the model. The lower scriber for marking soft materials is made by forcing a headless pin into a piece of dowel stock.

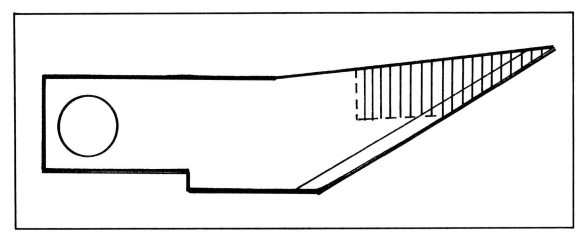

Fig. 3-5. A modified knife blade.

prices. To get started, the simple 5-or 10-pack is all right, or several modelers can share one of the bulk packs.

For cutting large circles in thin wood or paper, a *compass knife* is most effective. It's made from a small piece of sharpened steel and fits directly into the leg of a draftsman's compass in exactly the same fashion as an ordinary piece of pencil lead (Fig. 3-6). Don't skimp on quality for this item because less sturdy models will flex and bend under stress and not cut a true circle. Use only light pressure and make several passes to cut through. A large *wallpaper knife* with renewable blades is handy for cutting cardboard or insulation.

When there is a need for a large number of pieces of an identical length, it is almost impossi-

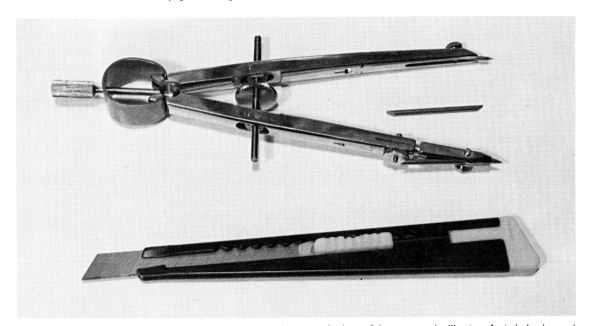

Fig. 3-6. A compass fitted with a steel knife edge (shown between the legs of the compass) will cut perfect circles in most light materials. An inexpensive wallpaper knife with a renewable blade is very helpful for rough cutting, such as cardboard or insulation.

ble to cut them individually. In this case I find it best to cut the individual pieces slightly oversize, then a clamp the pieces together, and sand down the ends at one time to the correct and identical length.

There are many units available for cutting wood to "exactly" the same length. One is a *chopper* (Fig. 3-7), an ordinary single-edged razor mounted in an arm mechanism that chops down across the wood piece. A metal stop mechanism allows the length to be cut repetitively. The stop on mine tends to drift a little; so I really clamp it down tight to prevent slipping. It may be my hand pressure or the way I pull down on the levers, but if you cut 10 pieces for the side of a cattle car that

must be exactly the same length, frankly they are not. The devices seem to cut smaller wood more successfully then larger sections beyond about 1/8 inch.

Master builder Charlie Dyxin, who has won *Model Railroader's* Model of the Month Award and national contest prizes several times showed me a simple little tool he built from scrap material to finish several pieces to exactly the same size after they come from one of the commercial cutters or after hand cutting. The device consists of a hand-held square block of wood with a piece of fine sand-paper glued to one face (Fig. 3-8). This slides along a second piece of wood, which acts as a little plat-form on a larger wood base. (Study the figures if

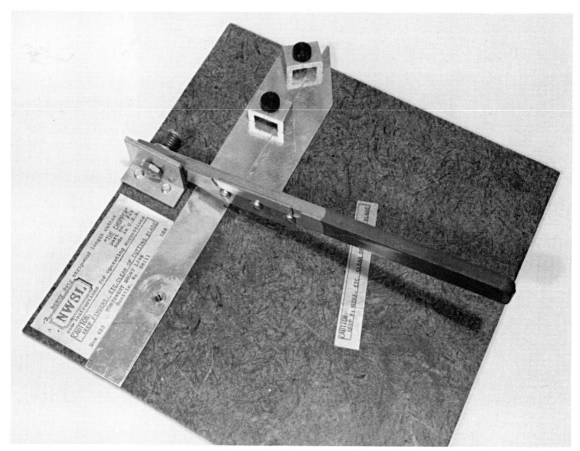

Fig. 3-7. The "chopper" is a commercial product available at most hobby shops. It will cut a number of copies of light wood to identical lengths. It is less effective for larger pieces.

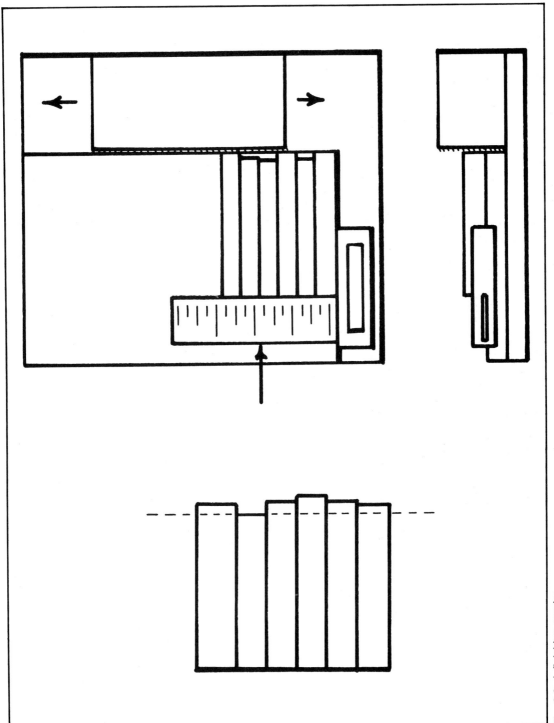

Fig. 3-8. A finishing sander.

this is getting confusing.) A small square is used to hold the rough-cut pieces upright, together, and square. By gentle hand pressure feed them into the sander which is being drawn back and forth with the other hand (Fig. 3-9). Kind of sounds like rubbing your tummy and patting your head at the same time, but it is a very effective tool for that fine finishing touch. The process only takes a few thousandths of an inch off the ends, but they are square and perfect.

Several manufacturers, including Dremel and Jarmac, make very nice disc sanders. They can be modified to do the same thing, but it's kind of like saddling a stallion when you need a gentle pony. With that much power, you're apt to take off too much, while with the Dyxin finishing sander, you'll get bored before you do any damage.

HOLDING TOOLS

For handling small pieces, you'll need a set of

Fig. 3-9. The sanding block on the left is slid slowly back and forth, while the square on the right feeds the pieces into the sander.

tweezers (Fig. 3-10). Actually think of them as an extension of your own fingers and use them often. Everything should be handled with tweezers, and as you become more familiar with them, this will be no problem. Tweezers come in many different kinds: fine points, plastic points, serrated, smooth, locking, and reverse styles. My advice is to use any kind with which you are comfortable. Probably the most important feature is the pressure needed to close the points. If they are just a little too stiff, your hand will tremble (perhaps imperceptibly) and make the tool hard to use. My own favorite tweezers are rather blunt with serrated tips, but they have just the right feel for me.

I also use several sets of clamping tweezers, called *hemostats,* for holding parts to be painted or filed. They protect my fingers from being abraded by the files and prevent serious cases of "modeler's fingers."

Several small *pliers*, usually a small needle-nose type, are handy. I especially recommend a set of round-nose jeweler's pliers for bending wire into eyelets, chain links, and curved sections. It's almost impossible to get a pure, round curvature without those special pliers (Fig. 3-11).

Several other types of clamps and holding devices are usually found around the modeler's shop. Large clamps can be used to hold pieces while the adhesive sets. Over the years I've collected several commercial types, including some very nice large metal clamps. My favorites, however, are plain old clothespins. For a little over a dollar, you can get a whole bag of these little goodies. The only major problem is that the tips are usually rounded and don't hold the model very well at tight fits. To improve their clamping action, I sand them on a belt sander to shape the tips in a variety of ways. Buy a bunch today and have some fun making your own clamps (Fig. 3-12).

Other inexpensive clamps are ordinary *rubber bands.* For curved or odd-shaped objects, they really can't be beat. With both the clothespins and rub-

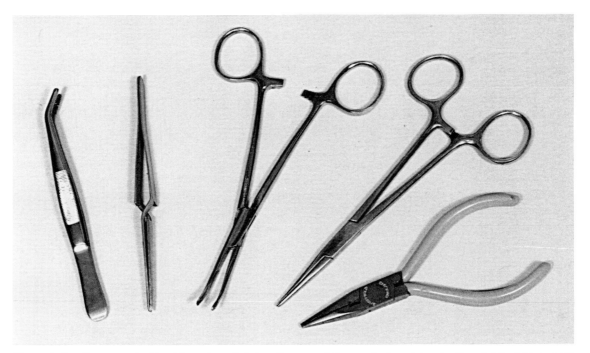

Fig. 3-10. Our fingers are just too big and rough to handle some of the smallest model parts. From left to right: a good set of tweezers with a very soft feel; reverse action or clamping tweezers (can be used for a very light clamp); two pairs of hemostats—one curved and one straight (with small locks on the handles, they make excellent clamps while painting or handling rather hard objects); a set of small pliers, which can be ground to different contours for special holding projects.

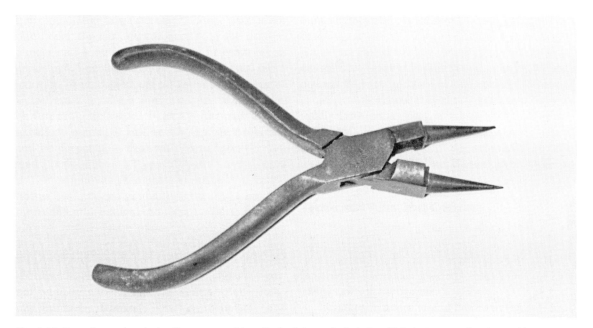

Fig. 3-11. Round nose jeweler's pliers are used to roll wire into perfect circles. This just cannot be done with a regular set of pliers. The cutters also can be used for cutting wire stock.

ber bands, I use just as many as necessary—don't skimp on your clamping power. One hint about rubber bands: when the glue has set, cut the rubber bands off with a very sharp razor rather than trying to roll or pull them off. You may lose a few rubber bands, but that is much better than tugging at them and possibly breaking the model.

If you can't clamp the pieces, then weights may be a good alternative. I use all kinds of metal stock cut offs, ranging from dime-size pieces to "Big Bertha"—a 10-pound monster cutoff used for large, laminated pieces of O-scale projects. A railroad spike makes a great weight for holding down car roofs because the head will hook over the roof peak, yet apply pressure. Some modelers use small bags of sand or lumps of lead, such as fishing weights. A lot of weight and plenty of patience will make for a very tight joint. Don't move your models too soon, but allow any type of adhesive to fully dry under the pressure of either clamps or weights.

Building cars is a bit different from making structures or other railroad artifacts. They tend to be fragile with many parts, both small and large, protruding from the basic body. We tend to finish the body then add the underbody detail and finally the trucks and couplers. I can't do much to change that sequence, but here are a couple of suggested holding devices, called *cradles*, to keep you from crushing those tiny grab irons while you attach the trucks, or from having the car constantly falling over while you put the grab irons on.

The first cradle is really a little platform used to hold the car upright without a set of trucks. Study Fig. 3-13. You can see the construction is very simple, using just four pieces of rather large stripwood that are glued together to form a little platform. This platform should be screwed directly to the bottom of the car in the same fashion as the trucks. The crosspieces must be large enough so that all the car underbody details—tanks, rods, and trussrods—will clear the base. I'd suggest that you attach one of these bases as soon as the basic car body is constructed. Doing so will allow you to work on the sides—doors, grab irons, etc.—by simply laying the car on its side.

The second type of cradle is a soft cloth basket (Fig. 3-14) which will hold a finished car without damaging details and allow you to work on the bottom or even the sides. This kind of holder is also useful for car repairs. Construction again is very simple, using two strips of wood—usually 1 × 2s in HO and maybe 2 × 4s in O scale—that are longer than your longest car, probably 80 scale feet. Use thumb tacks to string a piece of very thick soft cloth between the two side pieces. Not every car is the same size; so by moving the two pieces of wood back and forth, the size of the pocket can be changed and the pressure on the car modified. Once it is in place, the car can be worked on. Remember, though, this is not the time to hit it with a sledge-hammer. If major repairs are necessary, more drastic measures might be needed.

Fig. 3-12. Don't be afraid to use as many clothespins as you need for clamping.

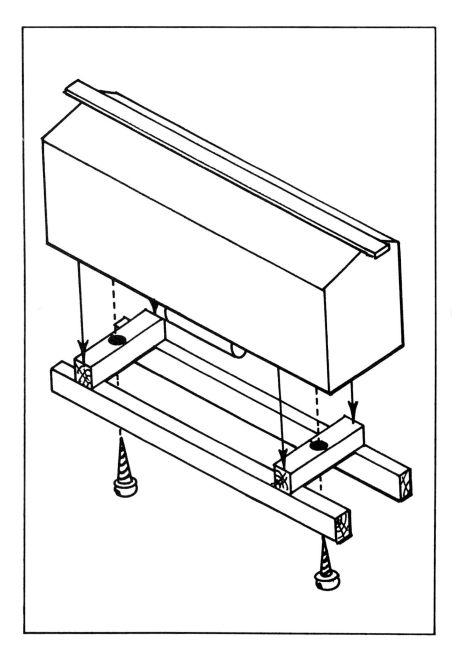

Fig. 3-13. A car platform.

FILING AND FINISHING TOOLS

For finishing metal, plastic, and even wood to a desired texture, *files* are most useful (Fig. 3-15). A few strokes of a sharp file may easily enlarge a slightly undersized opening. A round file is good for enlarging drill holes.

Files come in several different sizes and textures or face cuts. A small set of hobby (needle or pattern) files will easily satisfy most of your modeling needs. Select those with a sharp point. Manicuring emery boards may be substituted in some circumstances. For car sheathing in super-detailed models, a special sanding board may be made by

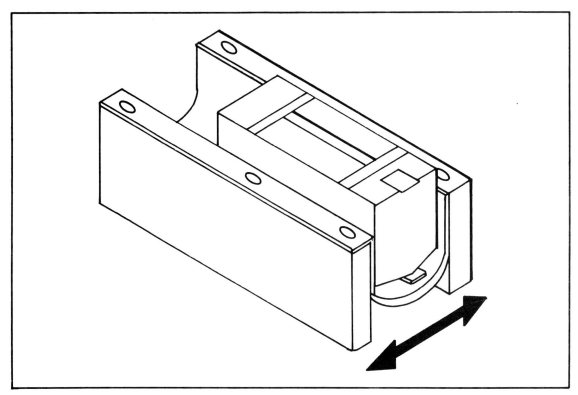

Fig. 3-14. A cloth cradle.

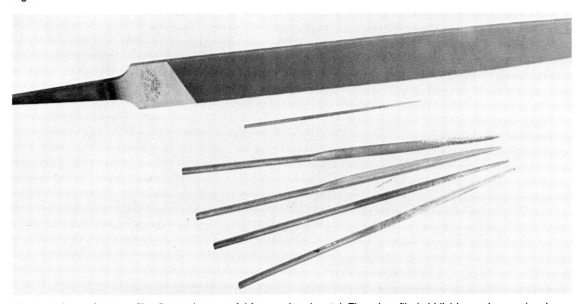

Fig. 3-15. A set of pattern files (bottom) are useful for wood and metal. The micro file (middle) has only occasional use, but when the clearances are very tight, there is no substitute. The large file with a mill face is good for removing large quantities of materials, including roughing out projects in wood and plaster.

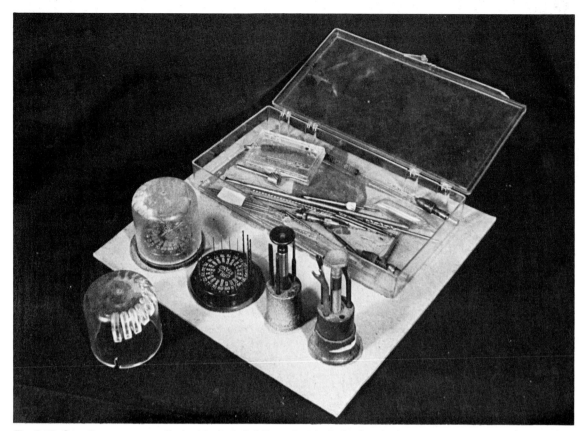

Fig. 3-16. Over the years you collect a lot of small drills and parts. I glued a plastic box, as well as small drill cases, a set of jeweler's screwdrivers, and wrenches to a piece of wood. Not all of this material is required for the beginning modeler—perhaps only a few of the wire-sized drills, depending on your scale, and pin vice or holder for the drills.

gluing sandpaper to a wooden stick of the appropriate size. Special curved files, called *riffles*, and micro-sized files may be purchased from the Brookstone Company. Finally, for rough sanding of very large pieces, one or two large mill-face or bastard-face files are handy.

Sandpaper is another way to finish surfaces. Various grades of abrasives are attached to either a paper or plastic backing. Commercial wet-or-dry 10- × -12-inch sheets available at hardware stores make a good starting point. Flex-i-grit packets with a mylar backing have sheets of many different grades and can be bent and flexed.

DRILLING TOOLS

A set of drills from 1/4 to 1/16 inch and graduated in 1/64 inches is the largest type of modeler will ever need. The *wire sizes,* or small drills from No. 60 to No. 80, are used more frequently by modelers and can be purchased in sets or individually. I have one complete set but find that I mainly use just a few. (Fig. 3-16) These, of course, are the ones that break the most often and need to be replaced. Pin vises may be used to hold the drills for hand boring. The tapered round minifile mentioned earlier may be used to expand the size of a hole, thus further limiting the need for many drills.

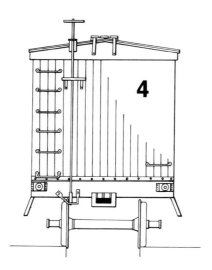

Safety and the Hobbyist

L IKE LOSING WEIGHT AND STOPPING EXCES-
sive charges on your credit cards, safety in
the home workshop is a subject we often talk about,
but somehow not much gets done. Unless we've experienced an accident or near-disaster, we just go
along hoping for the best. The secret is to make
safety a habit. I know that's a trite cliché, but it
is true. If you automatically reach for the safety
glasses before turning on the grinder or have taken
the time to make a spray booth for painting, the
danger of accidents is greatly reduced. Remember
if an accident can happen, it will . . . sooner or later.

The major areas of safety are chemicals (toxic
materials) and mechanisms (drills, knives, etc.). If
you operate a layout, electrical hazards are also
possible.

CHEMICAL HAZARDS

Perhaps the first advice I should give is that you
read the directions. Many new products are introduced to the model railroad field each year, and
no book can keep pace with them. The instructions
will alert you to possible hazards and safety procedures.

Prevention

It's also much better to prevent an accident
than to respond to one—that means keeping things
out of the reach of children. We have two inquisitive
sons, and one got some dye in his mouth. I rinsed
it out with 50,000 gallons of water, or at least it
seemed like that. I vowed never, never to leave a
chemical within reach of the children again. Now
that they are old enough to understand the danger
of chemicals, I openly show them how to use these
materials and instill, I hope, a fair sense of respect
for the danger. I was very pleased to find the entire collection of neighborhood kids in safety
glasses, ski goggles, and plastic shields to witness
my 10-year-old light a small "black snake"
fireworks piece on the 4th of July. This may have
been overkill, but it does show they are developing the habit.

Vapor Hazards

Back to the toxic materials. The first danger is from direct ingestion. If you've taken the precaution of keeping the paints, glues, and solvents away from the children, I will assume that you are not likely to drink Flouquil brush cleaner. The problem then is the vapors. Almost every bottle of paint or glue you buy says "Use with adequate ventilation." Seems like such an innocent statement, but what is "adequate ventilation?" Unfortunately I can't give a simple answer either. If there were a simple answer, they would print it on the label.

The problem is that when we breathe these chemicals, several factors must be considered. First is the concentration or level of exposure. Spraying an ounce of solvent into a barn-sized room may be perfectly safe, but spraying the same amount in a closet-sized workshop could be very hazardous. We need a lot of air to dilute the vapors. There are industrial hazard levels for almost every chemical we use. Unfortunately most modelers do not have the equipment or the know-how to measure and interpret these levels. At a high enough concentration, vapors can also explode from something as simple as the spark inside a wall switch or an electric motor. Although I know of no model shops exploding when you turn on the trains, it's still not good to have too much solvent around.

The second area is the length of exposure. The longer you are exposed to chemicals, even at low concentration, the greater are your chances of injury. Cap the bottle when you are not using it. If you must work with solvents, keep the time to several short periods, rather than one long one. Again there are standards for exposure, but most modelers are not prepared to log their times.

The third area is probably the most variable, and that is our own personal sensitivity to the materials. No matter what the toxicity charts say, I get headaches and a stuffy nose from even the smallest amounts of solvents in most commercial paints. These are the normal paint thinners found in the lacquers and enamels. You can buy various types of painting masks and filters, but they are almost exclusively designed to remove the small paint droplets and particles from the air, but not the chemical vapors. Unless the mask has canisters of charcoal or some specific agent designed to remove the solvent, it will be totally ineffective against the vapors.

Almost all of my model painting is done with Flouquil Polly S paints that are water-based, or with water-thinned household latex paints that have much lower solvent content. Where I must use a solvent-based paint, I use a small spray booth. It solves all the problems by sweeping away the paint particles and fumes with a small fan. Finding your own level of tolerance is important.

Spray Painting Hazards

For quality surface-coating, the airbrush is unsurpassed among modeling tools (Fig. 4-1). It leaves no brush marks, can apply exceedingly fine coats of paint, and is an effective tool for weathering and detailing. Airbrushing does require a certain amount of practice and experience, as well as investment in brush, compressor, valves, traps, etc., but the results are usually well worth it. It can be a real timesaver when you have a number of parts to paint or a particularly complicated and delicate model, like a styrene lace metalwork bridge or a hopper car with all the underbody details.

Along with the versatility, however, are some problems and hazards. Most modelers who use an airbrush do so in a commercial or homemade box sort of arrangement called a spray booth. The booth provides a convenient lighted work space, keeps paint from drifting all over the room, and removes solvent fumes. A wide variety of paints can be sprayed, including xylene and toluene-based rapid-drying paints and water-based acrylics. Most paints are thinned further with solvent for spraying. As the solvent vapors in the room build up during a long spraying session, they may eventually reach a dangerous level—the lower explosion limit (LEL). At this point any spark from perhaps a light switch, motor, or furnace pilot light can cause an explosion and rapid fire. Even at much lower levels, they may present a health hazard. For more detailed information, I asked Dave Methlie, a well-known model

Fig. 4-1. Custom builder Dave Methlie of Crystal Lake, Illinois, frequently makes use of an airbrush for painting models in his work.

railroad custom painter to share his spray painting suggestions.

The things we must do are to exhaust the solvent with a considerable volume of air and eliminate or reduce as far as possible exposure to ignition sources. These steps are accomplished by having a large fan exhaust the air in the booth to the outside usually through a furnace filter to trap the paint droplets. Typical range hoods without outside exhaust only recirculate the air minus particles and are totally unacceptable.

To ensure an adequate flow of air into a spray booth, the United States Environmental Protection Agency Air Pollution Engineering Manual AP-40 suggests a face or flow velocity of 100 to 200 feet per minute to prevent overspray from escaping and

to remove solvent vapors. For a particular spray booth, these air flow rates can be adjusted by choosing the proper size of fan rated in cubic feet per minute (cfm). The fan size may be computed from the following simple equation:

minimum: $\quad$ fan size (cfm) $= 100 \times A_f$
practical maximum: fan size (cfm) $= 200 \times A_f$

where A_f = area of the front of the booth in squarefeet.

Thus a small model type booth might be 1 1/2 feet high, 2 feet wide, and 2 feet deep. The minimum rated fan would then be:

fan size (cfm) $= 100 \times 1\ 1/2 \times 2 = 300$ cfm

The maximum necessary would be

$$\text{fan size (cfm)} = 200 \times 1\,1/2 \times 2 = 600 \text{ cfm}$$

Notice that the depth of the booth plays no part in the calculation. We've also assumed that the booth is relatively small and that the filter causes no drag or drop in air pressure. It's probably good practice to be a little on the high size rather than too low. As long as you work almost inside the booth, these flows will be satisfactory. For larger objects, however, it may be necessary to spray just outside and have the vapors pulled into the booth. The following equation would then apply.

$$\text{fan size (cfm)} = v_f \frac{(10X^2 + 2A_f)}{2}$$

where v_f = face velocity (100 to 200 fpm)
$\quad$ X = distance in feet to object from face of booth
$\quad$ A_f = area of front of booth in square feet

For example, if we wanted to spray as far as 2 feet in front of the same booth previously described and wanted maximum velocity of 200 fpm, the fan would then be sized by

$$\text{fan size (cfm)} = \frac{200\ 10\ (2)^2 + 2\ (1\,1/2 \times 2)}{2}$$

$$= 4600 \text{ cfm}$$

If you are confused by the math, just do the spraying inside the booth and use the simple equations.

The second problem is the possiblity of explosion caused by a spark. With a high air flow, vapors have little chance of building up, but it is still a good idea to isolate the booth from any source of sparks. Dave's booth, shown in Fig. 4-2, is a good example. Notice that all the electrical work is outside the booth in conduit. Even the light fixture is mounted outside with a sealed glass window to allow the illuminating light to pass through. The fan is mounted on top of the booth and has an explosion-proof motor. For model work, it's best to have the motor mounted as far from the air flow as possible. The body of this booth is wood, although sheet metal might make a lighter and more fire-resistant box.

I'm sure many modelers have been working for years without a booth or one that uses designs varying widely from what we have suggested. I wish them many years of successful hobbying. All I can say is an old bromide, "better safe than sorry."

Other Chemical Hazards

Should you splash or rub any chemical into your eye the best and, more importantly, the immediate treatment is flushing with large amounts of water, then getting immediate attention from a qualified physician. We deal with many different kinds of chemicals—solvents from paints, etching chemicals for brass, weathering chemicals, etc.—so it's impossible to suggest any treatment for each one. Try to keep the eye open while washing, which is difficult, and use a very gentle stream of water. Chemicals can do terrible things to your eyes; so good eye protection is best. A set of glasses or goggles should be the minimum for any machine operations that might involve flying materials or where chemicals might splash.

Be especially careful of the super glues, which can literally glue your eye closed instantly. The basic adhesives like white and yellow glues, pose little hazard since they are water-based and dry rather slowly. Epoxies and the thicker solvent glues, such as contact cement, do have solvents which evaporate and pose the same hazards as paint fumes. For years some people would sniff the solvent fumes to become light-headed. In many areas of the country, hobby cements will not be sold to minors. Some glues, such as the liquid plastic cements, are actually almost pure solvent and nearly completely evaporate form the work piece. These should be treated as paints for protection from fumes.

Probably the most dangerous are the super glues—ACC or cyanoacrylates. The fumes are very

Fig. 4-2. Dave Methlie's spray booth is an example of the best kind of safe constructions. The light and the switch are mounted outside the box, with illumination through a glass window on the top; the fan and the motor are mounted outside the box, and the fumes do not pass through the fan housing. Both of these features prevent an explosion from a spark should the solvent vapor build up too high. There is a cover for the both because cold air can enter through the vent. The compressor is directly underneath, and a full supply of paints is readily available. Models can be hand-held, but a small turntable inside the booth allows complete and easy turning.

irritating to the eyes, and instant bonding characteristics make no discrimination between hobby materials and your fingers and eyes. There are dissolving agents available, but it is possible to instantly glue your fingers together and need to have a physician surgically separate them. It's also very possible to just look into the end of a tube while trying to remove the frequent clogs that occur. One wrong move and a squirt of the super glue is in your eye and it instantly sets. Immediate action by a competent physician is absolutely essential. Use eye protection!

MECHANICAL HAZARDS

The other most common hazards are mechanical.

We use very sharp knives and drills; so the best protection is to always move the blade away from your hands and body. Just ask yourself, "What if the knife slips?" If it could hurt you, try another position, because some day it will slip and cut you. Finally when working around moving equipment, use safety glasses and remove all loose-fitting clothing or jewelry (Fig. 4-3). I personally have had a chunk of hair pulled out by getting too close to an uncovered pulley, and I own a set of plastic safety glasses with several large craters in them from chunks of hot metal thrown off by a large grinding wheel—better the glasses than my eyes.

There may be other potential hazards that are unique to your shop; so always be on guard. Once again, better safe than sorry.

SAFETY ON THE RAILS

Several times I've mentioned that there is no real substitute for prototype information. Although there are many books, plan packs, and publications available, sometimes that special car is just sitting there on the tracks or just over a hill in a yard waiting for you and your camera.

The first rule of prototype safety is never enter railroad property without permission. Railroads are private property, and technically you are a bona fide trespasser. Depending on the railroad's previous experience with rail fans and modelers, you may be escorted to the property line and summarily tossed out, or you may be escorted to the local police station to be locked up. The second possibility is rare, but I wouldn't want to walk onto

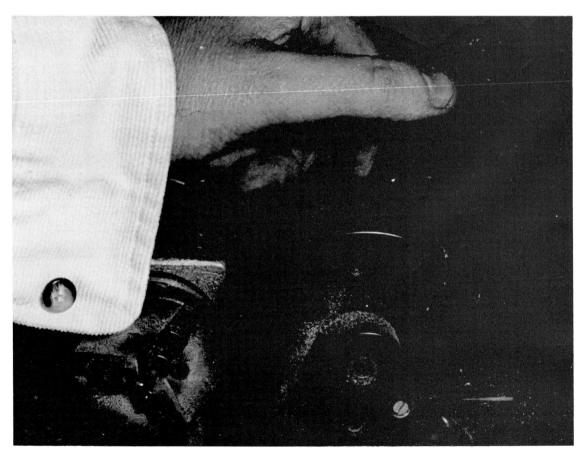

Fig. 4-3. When the lathe is rotating, a loose cuff or long hair can easily be caught in the machinery, dragging your hand or head into the whirling metal. Always confine loose clothing and hair and wear eye protection.

a site just after vandals had derailed a train or caused some serious form of damage.

If you cannot write ahead to the corporate headquarters for permission, the yardmaster's office, section house, or station is a good place to start. I try to be very straightforward, starting with something about my interest in trains and that I pose no potential problem to the railroad. You know in these days of instant lawsuits, anyone with a camera wandering around taking pictures is a real threat. Permission may include signing a release which absolves the company of liability in case of injury. This is not a license for stupidity since you are now responsible for your own safety.

My basic outfit includes a long-sleeved work shirt and heavy work pants. A railroad yard is a dirty place; so there's no sense in ruining good clothing. I have a pair of heavy work boots with reinforced toes. Street shoes are inappropriate when you might step on a spike, sharp wire, or the like.

I have a hard hat borrowed from my Dad. This may seem like overkill, but I can still remember being in the cab of a steam engine at Northwestern Steel and Wire Company. A second engine was switching nearby, and I quickly started to move from one side of the cab to the other only to run smack into a solid steel pipe protruding from the engine. Except for the hard hat provided by the company to visitors, I would have had a large gash in my head.

Other advice: never release valves, try to move equipment, or climb too high on stationary cars. You cannot be sure they will not be subject to switching at some time when you are not ready. Watch out for moving trains. While you are engrossed in setting up a shot or measuring a car, a second train can sneak up on you. Especially in the din of a railyard, you just may not hear the second train.

Never judge the distance to a train looking through your viewfinder on the camera. The image can be deceivingly small and be much closer than you expect.

Don't back up while looking through the camera. Get in the habit of taking the camera down, looking behind you, stepping back, planting your feet, then returning to the camera. It may sound silly, but many modelers have tripped over an adjacent track, fallen down a drainage ditch, or worse. Don't spoil your trip with an accident.

One of my most pleasant memories is that of spending a Sunday afternoon in the Mendota, Illinois, interlocking tower with Editor Bill Schaumburg of *Railroad Model Craftsman*, just watching the parade of trains roll by on the IC and CB&Q. That is what railroads are all about. Good safety habits can keep it that way.

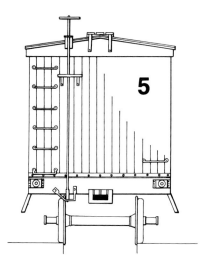

Reading Plans and Blueprints

ROBABLY IN NO OTHER AREA OF MODEL
railroading are plans and blueprints more important than in building cars. The more elaborate and detailed the car, the more we need to know about its construction as shown in plans. You need not be a mechanical engineer with a PhD to enjoy scratchbuilding and modifying kits; so skim through this chapter to get basic ideas. If you are simply uninterested in plans, go on to trying kitbashing or other projects. Maybe after getting the feel for building a few cars, you'll come back and view this chapter differently.

SCALE AND GAUGE

Up until this point I've made no mention of either scale or gauge. The basic construction arts of cutting, gluing, and sanding are really without scale. For building cars, however, scale is very important, and gauge can make a real difference. All models are built to a predetermined *scale*, or reduced proportion of the original.

The scales range from the largest—O scale—to the smallest—Z scale (Figs. 5-1 and 5-2). The once predominant O scale of 1/4 inch = 1 foot, or a proportion of 1/48 (that is, the models are 1/48th the size of the prototype) has been replaced in popularity by HO (Half O) with a scale of 3.5 millimeters = 1 foot, or a proportion of 1 to 87 (that is the models are about 1/87th the size of the prototype).

O scale is the largest of the popular scales and offers the chance to highly detail almost massive models. Many contest winners are modeled in O scale because of the ease in detailing. Because of their size, O-scale rolling stock usually track very well and have a prototype feel about them. They can, to some degree, make up for track work that is less than perfect. The main disadvantage of O scale is the huge space required for even a small layout. Long passenger cars may require a track radius of 48 or even 60 inches. Cars and locomotives can be expensive, with a good imported brass engine ranging well beyond $1000. Many O-

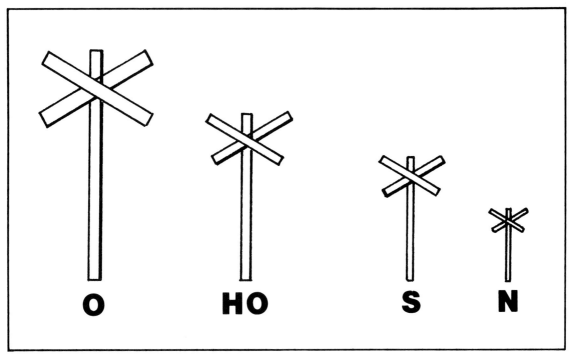

Fig. 5-1. Model scales shown to scale.

Fig. 5-2. Here you can see the comparative sizes of an O-, HO-, and N-scale model.

scale modelers choose to scratchbuild and avoid the high costs. O scale has two newsletters dedicated to it's followers—*O Scale News* and *O Scale Railroading* (see the Appendix).

The popularity of HO scale can be credited to the moderate space required with still a good potential for detailing. A huge variety of kits and ready-to-run equipment makes HO an excellent scale for modelers of all skill levels.

N scale is the smallest popular scale at 1.9 millimeters = 1 foot, or a proportion of 1 to 160. The small size makes for a lot of railroad in a very small space. If you like long trains, yards full of cars, and plenty of scenery all on a coffee table, then N scale is for you. There are several scratchbuilders in this scale, and it's just amazing what can be done even at these tiny proportions.

For those interested in a compromise between the size of O scale and the convenience of HO, modelers might look to S scale, at 3/16 inch = 1 foot, or a proportion of 1 to 64. The scale allows for plenty of detailing, yet doesn't require the space or expense of O scale. Although in a clear minority, there is a growing following of S scale with a full list of manufacturers and specialty suppliers, mostly by mail (see the Appendix). That favorite American Flyer train you had around the Christmas tree was S scale. Reading one of the S-gauge newsletters like the *S Gaugian*, you will find that there is a flourishing business in trading, selling, repairing,

and operating much of the original S-gauge equipment.

In addition to the scales already mentioned, there are a number of other modeling proportions, both larger and smaller; so everyone can find his or her own niche. Tables 5-1 and 5-2 list the major scales, proportions, and conversions.

In dealing with cars, we must also add some discussion about gauge. In common usage, the words gauge and scale are often interchanged as in "O Gauge" or "HO Gauge." In reality, *gauge* refers to the spacing between the rails of the prototype track. The standard spacing, or standard gauge, is 4 feet 8 1/2 inches. In the early history of railroading, each railroad company built tracks to their own specifications, ranging from gauges of 5 feet to as small as 2 feet. Of course this caused tremendous confusion and resulted in both freight and passengers having to frequently switch cars and trains at interchange points. The railroads finally agreed on the standard 4 feet 8 1/2 inches. There were, however, plenty of holdouts, usually among the narrower gaugers in mining and logging areas. The smaller gauge proved an advantage in that it could be quickly constructed, required less excavation, and used smaller cars and locomotives, which could climb steeper hills and round sharper curves. Even today, remnants of the narrower gauge systems can be found. The Quincy and Torch Lake 3-foot gauge copper mining railroad in Hancock,

Table 5-1. Model Railroading Scales and Proportions.

NAME OF SCALE	SCALE TO FOOT	PROPORTION	CENTER OF COUPLER ABOVE TOP OF RAIL	TRACK GAUGE
O	¼″	1:48	11/16″ (17mm)	1.250″ (31.76mm)
S	3/16″	1:64	17/32″ (13.5mm)	0.875″ (22.23mm)
OO	4mm (0.157″)	1:76.2	29/64″ (11.5mm)	0.750″ (19.00mm)
HO	3.5mm (0.138″)	1:87.1	25/64″ (9.9mm)	0.650″ (16.50mm)
TT	1/10″	1:120	9/32″ (7.1mm)	0.471″ (11.97mm)
N	1.9mm (0.075″)	1:160	0.216″ (5.5mm)	0.354″ (9.00mm)
Z	1.38mm (0.0544″)	1:220		0.256″ (6.50mm)

Table 5-2. Model Railroading Conversion Chart.

	O	S	00	HO	TT	N	Z
O	1	.750	.630	.551	.400	.300	.218
S	1.333	1	.840	.735	.553	.400	.290
00	1.585	1.190	1	.875	.635	.476	.346
HO	1.815	1.360	1.143	1	.725	.544	.396
TT	2.500	1.875	1.575	1.377	1	.750	.545
N	3.333	2.500	2.100	1.837	1.333	1	.727
Z	4.583	3.437	2.887	2.526	1.833	1.375	1

Michigan (Fig. 5-3), and the operating 3-foot gauge railroads such as the East Broad Top in Orbisonia, Pennsylvania, and the descendents of Denver and Rio Grande Western Railroad in Durango, Colorado, are all examples. You can even ride 2-foot narrow gauge trains from the once extensive Sandy River and Rangley Lake Railroad in Maine at Edaville railroad near Boston.

To build a model of one of the Quincy Mining Company Gondolas in HO scale and report this is an HO gauge car really is confusing and incorrect. Actually the car would be built to HO proportion for use on 3-foot gauge tracks. A shorthand notation is used in this case—HOn3—meaning HO scale is used for cars, locomotives, buildings, people, etc., but the wheels on the rolling stock are spaced 3 feet apart. Other examples are Nn2, On3, and HOn3 1/2, etc.

Because the surviving narrow-gauge railroads usually were isolated, self-sufficient, and independent to the very end, they frequently used homemade, unusual, and very interesting types of cars, attracting many of the very best modelers.

PLANS AND DRAWINGS

If a picture is worth a thousand words, then a plan is worth a million. Nothing conveys as much information to the modeler as a good set of scale plans. There are many sources of plans, including the popular model magazines and books. They are drawn in an easy-to-understand pictorial style that shows the entire car exterior from several different views, and they are excellent places to begin your career as a car builder (Figs. 5-4 and 5-5). In general, the larger the drawing appears, the easier it is to use. I generally like the large O-scale drawings even if they must be converted into a smaller scale for actual building. Magazine draftsmen make their drawings in 3/8-inch scale or larger, which are then reduced photographically by the printer. As the size goes down, however, so does your ability to read and transfer the dimensions. Look for the largest-sized drawings possible.

Two additional problems with magazine drawings are French shading and printing error. Examine a drawing in a magazine carefully (even mine in this book) and you'll see that some of the lines are darker or actually thicker than others. This is called *French shading* and gives the drawings a slight shadow or three-dimensional effect. At the same time, it is more difficult to locate the end of the line, especially if the shading is heavy. Engineering drawings usually have uniform thin lines to avoid this problem.

There is also a slight printing error in most magazines ranging to 3 to 5 percent. This is not as noticeable in the larger scales, but becomes more important in the smaller scales. Find a drawing of a long passenger car in HO or N scale, especially if it crosses the magazine spine. Place your scale rule under the car and compare it to the printed dimension. A 60-foot car may be in error by as much as 1.5 scale feet. One solution would be to have the plans copied and adjusted by a blueprint house, but I'm willing in many cases to have a little less accurate model than to go through all the trouble to correct it. Just be aware of the problems and be prepared to deal with them however you wish.

After following the plans in kits and in hobby magazines, you can graduate to the best source of modeling information: prototype plans. Usually super-detailed, these plans deviate significantly from the common magazine plans. First, the construction firm was interested in far more than the exterior; so the side view will usually be only partial exteriors with several cut-away sections showing interiors, framing, bracing, couplers, and supports. The location of a cut-away section frequently is indicated by letters and arrows, such as section AA, BB, AC, etc. End views are especially confusing where one side of the view may show the end of the car, while the other side is a view at the center of the car or other important location (Fig. 5-6). It takes some time to study these plans with all their information, but the task is usually worth it. I'd much rather have too much information and not use some than to have too little.

A number of excellent reprints of actual prototype drawings can be found in Newton Gregg's Train Shed series of reprints. These are short, paperbound books taken from old prototype Cyclopedias and reference books. They are usually sections of several books referring to the same material, such as boxcars of the 1940s, passenger cars of the 1920s, etc. I've reviewed some of the more modern Cyclopedias, but they contain only a few plans that are schematic rather than detailed (Fig. 5-7). Other sources of actual railroad plans are historical societies, both local and national, and private collections. It's sometimes amazing how friendly and willing to share other modelers are if you just ask! Local meetings of such groups as the National Model Railroad Association and rail historical groups (see Appendix) are good places to

hunt down some plans. Don't be surprised to find drawings scaled at 1/2 inch = 1 foot or even larger. These are called *erection drawings* and really show detail! Don't expect instant results, but be persistent and be prepared to pay a fair price. One of my projects took almost 10 years to complete but was finally finished because of a lunch-time conversation with another modeler who happened to have a set of blueprints from the original prototype builder. Luck? A little bit. Persistence? Yes!

Types of Prints and Copying

Original drawings might be available in one of many forms. Very old master drawings were drawn in ink on linen content cloth and survived surprisingly well. I copied a linen-based drawing from the 1860s with little trouble.

Modern masters would be drawn on mylar or other dimensionally stable plastic-based material. Copies from both linen and mylar are made by placing a sheet of photo-sensitive material directly in contact with the master and then passing the sandwich through a machine that shines light on the pair. The exposed sheet is separated from the master and passed through some developing agent— frequently ammonia fumes—which makes the familiar blue or brown line prints. The process can also be adjusted to make blueprints, where the copies have white lines with a nearly full blue background. This kind of copying is fast and inexpensive.

Many times you will not be lucky enough to find an original linen, but have only a blueline or blueprint. Copying these is more expensive because a photographic copy must be made to create a negative, which in turn is used to make prints. An advantage, though, is that once a negative has been made, it is possible to change the scale of the final print. Since many blueprint shops do not understand what our O, HO, and S scales mean, I find it best to give them very specific instructions based on the final size of the drawing I want. For example I might give the written instructions "reduce the full length of the car (mark this on the drawing) to exactly 10 inches" (this is correct for a

Fig. 5-3. A lonely caboose stands outside the Quincy enginehouse in the late 1970s.

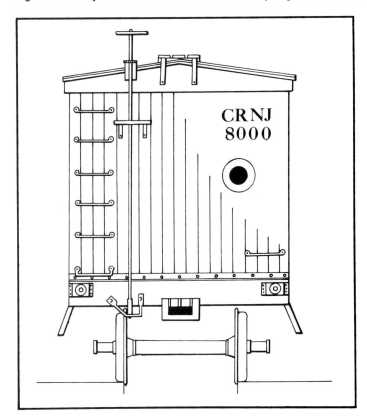

CRNJ
8000

Fig. 5-4. The front view of a car (O scale).

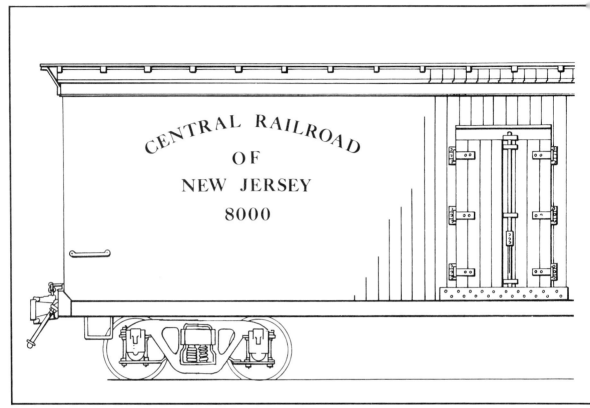

Fig. 5-5. Side view of the car (O scale).

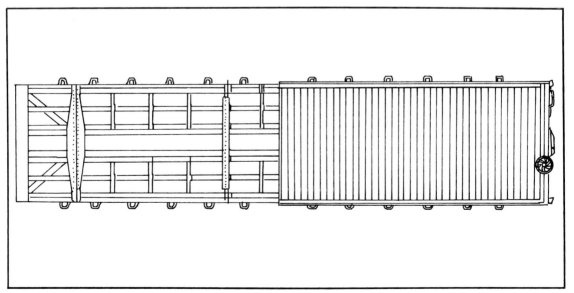

Fig. 5-6. A cutaway view (not to scale).

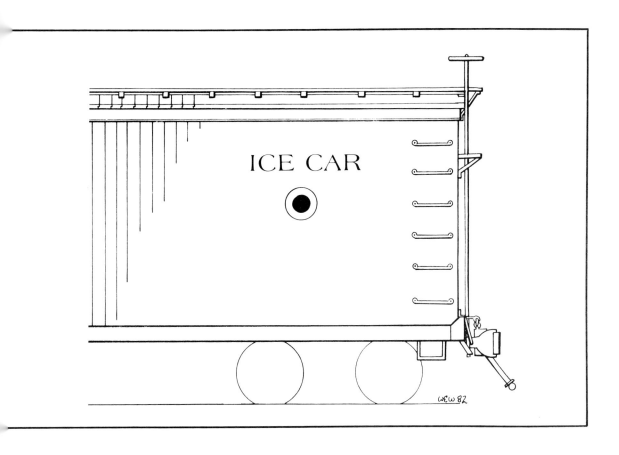

40-foot O-scale car). After working with a shop for awhile, you will be able to communicate better and minimize the reduction problems. Nothing really beats a scale drawing in your own scale.

Office copying machines can be used for rapid and inexpensive copying. The darkness, quality, and dimensions will vary some among machines—some good and some very bad. It's always a good

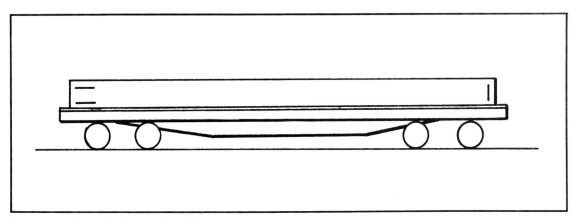

Fig. 5-7. A schematic view (not to scale).

idea to test the machine with a copy of a piece of graph paper or a ruler itself and then measure the image on the copy.

To read the drawings, you can purchase an inexpensive engineer's or architect's rule, which will give you 1/4 inch, 1/2 inch, 1 inch, and other common larger scales.

Making Your Own Plans

Many times commercial plans are not available for a particular project. Making your own plans, or at least getting basic dimensions down on paper, isn't that hard. Probably the first thing to realize is that you are probably not a professional draftsman or architect and that the finished product you make should be good for building purposes but not ready to hang on a gallery wall. With the notion of perfection out of the way, drawing a simple plan becomes a lot easier. I suggest a two-fold attack:

simple photography and basic sketching.

Using whatever type of camera you have available, take a number of inexpensive black-and-white photographs of your prototype. Basic shots should be directly straight on from each side and end (Fig. 5-8). If the car is quite long, you may have to take several shots walking along the car, but always try to stay straight on. These will not make especially artistic photographs, but they keep all the edges parallel. Take a number of close-up and detail photographs just for the record. Remember film is really cheap, but returning many miles to try to find a special car can be more than difficult. If you have a 35mm camera, taking a set of color slides of the main sides of the car will also be helpful.

Once the photos are safely in the camera, out comes a note pad and a tape measure. Having a friend along to help is very useful. My sons have

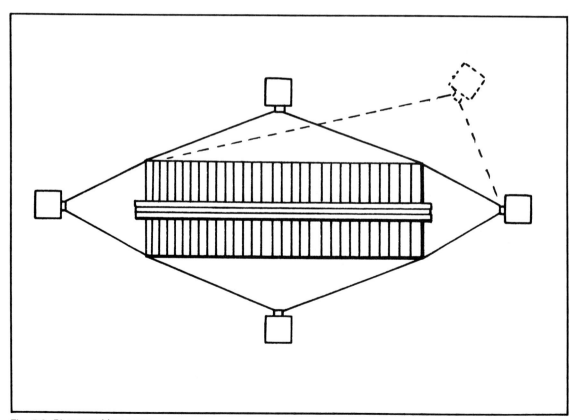

Fig. 5-8. Photographing a car.

Fig. 5-9. Son Tony demonstrates how to reach up with a carpenter's rule.

found this a great adventure with dad. You can measure everything possible, but begin just with the basics. Draw a simple box and record length, width, and height. Be very careful about climbing up on equipment. Sometimes it's better to estimate heights rather than take a chance on being injured. No model is worth an accident. I use a 100-foot metal tape measure to get the long dimensions and an 8-foot folding carpenter rule for short dimensions

and for reaching up on a car (Fig. 5-9). Since the ruler doesn't flex, I can reach up 13 feet or more. From the basic dimensions and the photograph details, you should easily be able to locate all the parts and build the basic car.

An easy alternative to all the measuring and drawing is to use the projection drawing method. First, tape a large piece of drawing paper on the wall. On the paper mark two lines at the exact scale

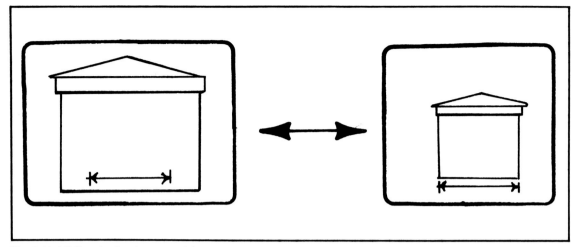

Fig. 5-10. Wall projection (not to scale).

length of your car. Choose any scale you like, but again the larger the better. Now project a side-view 35mm slide of your car onto the paper. By moving the projector back and forth while adjusting the focus, you should be able to project an image of the car of exactly the correct length onto the paper (Fig. 5-10). When you get as correct an image as possible, use a dark pencil or marker to mark the important locations—doors, windows, trim, roof contours. Remember, this is not a Rembrandt, but just a locator of details. The castings and parts you add to the final car will carry the details. Once the basic drawing is made, you're off to the workshop to begin building just as we do in the projects in this book.

Scaling Photographs

Many times all you have to work from is an old photograph or maybe only your own photographs. The thought of drawing a set of plans is the last thing you want to do. Well don't give up hope; there is a way to make a simple ruler that is scaled exactly for your photograph. Again you begin with the flat or straight-on views of the photograph. You need only one dimension—probably the longest car dimension. The problem is to make a special ruler marked off in units exactly equal to that longest dimension. Here's how to do it.

If you have a photograph of a 10-foot car end,

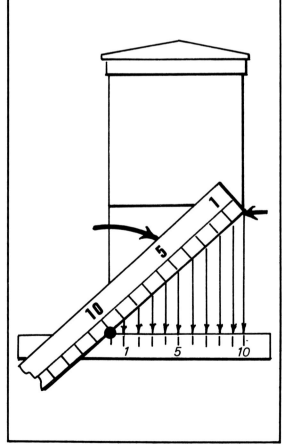

Fig. 5-11. Scaling a photograph.

as in Fig. 5-11, mark the length of the car on a piece of graph paper. Then take a ruler (any size will do, but it must be longer than the actual car photograph) and locate 10 units on the ruler (1/8ths, 1/4ths, or 1/10ths). Locate the 10th unit of the ruler at one edge of the car and pivot the ruler until the 1st unit is directly above the end of the line. By dropping lines down at each of the units, a scale with 10 units exactly the width of your car end is created. This same scale can then be used to measure any other dimension on the photograph. You will have to make a new scale for each photograph. The same method can be used to make an instant scale for any flat-view photograph.

It is possible to scale the classic 3/4-construction view, but that is beyond the basics I am describing in this book. You might consult a good book on engineering graphics for the interpretation of these orthographic projections.

Summary

Well I hope you have seen that there are many kinds, styles, and types of plans. Some will give you more information than you can use, while others may be just the basic dimensions. The important thing, however, is to get some plans and jump into your own scratchbuilding or super-detailing projects—that's when the fun begins.

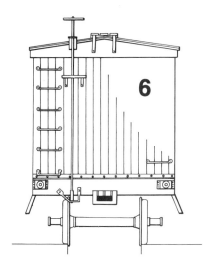

Working With Wood

WOOD OF SOME VARIETY HAS BEEN AVAIL-
able worldwide for centuries. Several thousand years ago Egyptians modeled wooden boats
for the tombs of their Pharoahs. Today wood is still
used extensively for models of all types. It can be
easily cut and carved, glued and stained. It can be
made to stimulate almost anything, including concrete and metal, but wood works best looking like
wood.

Railroads used wood for building, ties, and rolling stock from the beginning. The older and more
rural the railroad, the more likely was the use of
wood. Frequently millions of board feet of timber
were harvested from local forests to create giant
trestles.

Today model companies are producing
packaged urethane and polyester plastics, metal,
and even plaster kits to be finished to look like
wood. Of course, using model wood with stains and
paint to simulate aged, weathered wood is easy. In
using strips of wood to produce a model boxcar,
gondola, stock car, or even caboose, the builder can
use prototype construction techniques with almost
board-by-board construction.

In examining an old or aging prototype car, you
will notice the variety in the color and texture of
each board. Different boards weather and age at
different rates. Some have extra-coarse grain and
knotholes, while others are smooth. These variations can easily be simulated by building up your
structures from boards that are prestained varying
colors and then scrambled and mixed before construction. I will talk more on this topic later.

TYPES OF WOOD

Timber used in manufacturing covers a wide range
of wood types, but in the modeling hobby, we are
basically limited to three types: balsa, pine, and
basswood.

Balsa is a very light, open-grained wood that
is frequently used to make model airplanes because
of its lightness. It is difficult to cut, however, and
crushes easily under the pressure of a knife. Paint-

ing and staining balsa is most difficult, since it seems to have an insatiable thirst. It is not a major wood for the serious model railroader.

Clear *pine* is frequently used by kit manufacturers for large blocks, such as the ends and bases of boxcar kits. It is denser and harder than basswood, and although it cuts easily with a power saw, it is difficult to cut with modeling tools. It is generally available at better lumber yards, but it is not recommended for use by the novice modeler.

Basswood is the lightest of the hardwoods and is virtually the sole wood used by major kit and material manufacturers. Basswood is more difficult to carve than cherry or walnut because it is so light. It also tends to split rather easily along its grain. Perhaps its most annoying characteristic is the unpleasant surface grain, or fuzz, that leaps up upon the application of paint or stain. In addition, large pieces cut on a power saw will easily burn if the blade is not razor sharp.

Still, despite all these difficulties, basswood is the best available modeling wood. It is hard enough to hold its shape and provide sufficient strength for the model, while exhibiting a fine grain and good paint-holding characteristics. It's also soft enough to cut with most modeling tools. As we go along, I will point out ways to simplify your use of basswood to overcome its shortcomings.

WOOD STOCK

Wood supplies for the modeler come in a variety of formats. The most crude are the basswood sheets and large blocks from cabinetmakers' supply shops. Sheets range from 1/8 × 5 inches up to regular 2 × 4s. Turning blocks are usually several inches square. The price per foot or pound of wood is quite low, but you have a lot of work to do before you can use it for a model. Some modelers, especially those who work in larger scales, will start with this stock and cut smaller pieces on a power saw. I use a special saw hole plate, but those techniques are beyond the scope of this book. As you develop your interest and skills, and your need for very large quantities of cut wood increases, it might be an area you'll want to further investigate.

Stripwood

Many manufacturers cut basswood down to certain common fractional sizes, such as 1/8 × 1/16 inch or 1/4 × 3/32 inch. These pieces are generally called *stripwood* and are usually sold in lengths up to 24 inches, but not related to any particular scale or gauge. Simply use those pieces that are closest to your appropriate scale dimensions. (See Table 6-1.)

Scale Lumber

Several manufacturers have commercially available basswood machined to scale lumber sizes; that is actual 2 × 4s or 2 × 12s correctly dimensioned for your scale (Fig. 6-1). This type of material is currently available primarily for modelers in HO and O scale, but other scales are beginning to be supplied as well. These are rough-sized lumber pieces, not finished lumber; so a 2 × 4 is actually 2 scale inches by 4 scale inches, while the piece of lumber you buy in the lumberyard is not a 2 × 4, but is actually finished down just slightly to about 1 3/4 × 3 3/4 inches. In all but the largest scales and most exacting models, this will make little difference.

There are, however, no rules that you must use only O scale lumber if you model in O scale. I frequently jump between HO, O, and stripwood sizes to find the piece of lumber that is most suited to the work I am doing at the moment. For example, the little crosspieces in a window, called *muntins*, are about 3/4 × 1/2 inch. While no O scale piece is available, and HO 1 × 2 easily fits the bill. To help you in selecting the correct lumber size for the job, I've developed simple conversion tables for all the currently available lumber and stripwood sizes. They are shown in Tables 6-2 and 6-3.

Structural and Specialty Shapes

In addition to the selection of lumber and stripwood, also available are a number of different structural shapes and forms in wood. They include items like H-columns, I-beams, Z-braces, dowels, quarter rounds, door track, and channels. Properly finished, they can simulate metal for those who don't

Table 6-1. HO Scale and Fractional Lumber Sizes.

ACTUAL SIZE	COMPARISON SIZE	O	S	00	HO	TT	N	Z
0.0115	1″ (HO)	½	¾	⅞	1	1⅜	1⅞	2½
0.0208	1″ (O)	1	1⅜	1⅝	1¾	2½	3⅜	4⅝
0.0230	2″ (HO)	1⅛	1½	1¾	2	2¾	3⅝	5
0.0312	1/32″	1½	2	2⅜	2¾	3¾	5	6⅞
0.0344	3″ (HO)	1⅝	2¼	2⅝	3	4⅛	5½	7½
0.0394	1mm	1⅞	2½	3	3⅜	4¾	6¼	8⅝
0.0417	2″ (HO)	2	2⅝	3⅛	3⅝	5	6⅝	9⅛
0.0459	4″ (HO)	2¼	3	3½	4	5½	7⅜	10⅛
0.0469	¾	2¼	3	3½	4	5⅝	7½	10¼
0.0625	1/16″ & 3″ (O)	3	4	4¾	5½	7½	10	13¾
0.0689	6″ (HO)	3¼	4⅜	5¼	6	8¼	11	15⅛
0.0781	5/64	3¾	5	6	6¾	9⅜	12½	17¼
0.0833	4″ (O)	4	5⅜	6⅜	7¼	10	13⅜	18⅜
0.0916	8″ (HO)	4⅜	5⅞	7	8	11	14¾	20¼
0.0938	3/32	4½	6	7⅛	8⅛	11¼	15	20⅝
0.1148	10″ (HO)	5½	7⅜	8¾	10	13¾	18⅜	25¼
0.1250	⅛ & 6″ (O)	6	8	9½	10⅞	15	20	27½
0.1378	12″ (HO)	6⅝	8⅞	10½	12	16½	22	30¼
0.1560	5/32	7½	10	11⅞	13⅝	18¾	25	34⅜
0.1608	14″ (HO)	7¾	10¼	12¼	14	19¼	25¾	35⅜
0.1667	8″ (O)	8	10⅝	12¾	14½	20	26⅝	36⅝
0.1837	16″ (HO)	8⅞	11¾	14	16	22	29⅜	40⅜
0.1880	3/16	9	12	14½	16⅜	22½	30	41¼
0.1970	5mm	9½	12⅝	15	17⅛	23⅝	31½	43¼
0.2067	18″ (HO)	9⅞	13¼	15¾	18	24¾	33	45½
0.2083	10″ (O)	10	13⅜	15⅞	18⅛	25	33⅜	45⅞
0.2296	20″ (HO)	11	14¾	17½	20	27½	36¾	50½
0.2500	¼ & 12″ (O)	12	16	19	21¾	30	40	55
0.2526	22″ (HO)	12⅛	16⅛	19¼	22	30¼	40⅜	55½
0.2756	24″ (O)	13¼	17⅛	21	24	33	44	60⅝
0.2917	14″ (O)	14	18⅝	22¼	25⅜	35	46⅝	64⅛
0.3120	5/16	15	20	23¾	27¼	37½	50	68¾
0.3333	16″ (O)	16	21⅜	25⅜	29	40	53⅜	73⅜
0.3750	⅜ & 18″ (O)	18	24	28⅝	32⅝	45	60	82½
0.3940	10mm	18⅞	25¼	30	34¼	47¼	63	86⅝
0.4167	20″ (O)	20	26⅝	31¾	36¼	50	66⅝	91⅝
0.4380	7/16	21	28	33⅜	38	52½	70	96¼
0.4583	22″ (O)	22	29⅜	34⅞	39⅞	55	73⅜	100⅞
0.5000	½ & 24″ (O)	24	32	38⅛	43½	60	80	110
0.7500	¾	36	48	57⅛	65¼	90	120	165
1.0000	1	48	64	76¼	87⅛	120	160	220

All dimensions given in scale inches to nearest ⅛ of a scale inch.

These handy tables offer a quick means to convert strip-wood sizes to scale lumber dimensions, or convert scale lumber sizes from one scale to another

like to work with a soldering gun. Remember to be careful when cutting and working with these very fragile materials.

Sheet Stock

Individually gluing on every board of a stock car or boxcar may be too overwhelming a thought

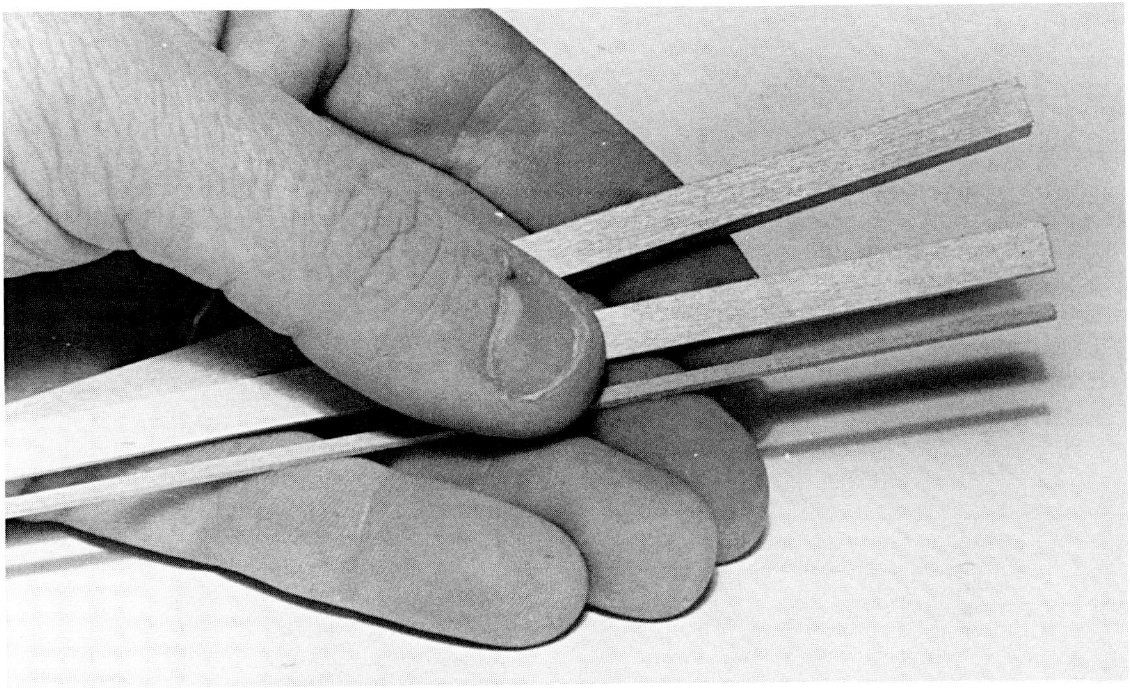

Fig. 6-1. Scale lumber comes in long sizes. From the top to the bottom are a scale 6 × 12, 2 × 12, and 2 × 4.

for many people. Premilled siding in a variety of styles may be just the answer you are seeking. Thin sheets, usually 1/32 or 1/16 inch thick and 2 to 4 inches wide, have a structural surface milled into them. Various styles include clapboard, planking, random planking, and board and batten, among others. They are most useful for models with large surface areas.

SELECTING AND STORING WOOD

Anyone who is at all serious about scratchbuilding should begin now to build up a virtual lumberyard

Table 6-2. O Scale Lumber.

O	S		OO		HO		TT		N		Z	
1	1.33	1 3/8	1.59	3/4	1.81	1 3/4	2.50	2 1/2	3.33	3 3/8	4.58	4 5/8
2	2.67	2 5/8	3.18	3 1/8	3.63	3 5/8	5.00	5	6.67	6 5/8	9.17	9 1/8
3	4.00	4	4.76	4 3/4	5.44	5 1/2	7.50	7 1/2	10.00	10	13.75	13 3/4
4	5.33	5 3/8	6.35	6 3/8	7.26	7 1/4	10.00	10	13.33	13 3/8	18.33	18 3/8
6	8.00	8	9.52	9 1/2	10.88	10 7/8	15.00	15	20.00	20	27.50	27 1/2
8	10.67	10 5/8	12.70	12 3/4	14.51	14 1/2	20.00	20	26.67	26 5/8	36.67	36 5/8
10	13.33	13 3/8	15.88	15 7/8	18.14	18 1/8	25.00	25	33.33	33 3/8	45.83	45 7/8
12	16.00	16	19.05	19	21.77	21 3/4	30.00	30	40.00	40	55.00	55
14	18.67	18 5/8	22.22	22 1/4	25.40	25 3/8	35.00	35	46.67	46 5/8	64.17	64 1/8
16	21.33	21 3/8	25.40	25 3/8	29.03	29	40.00	40	53.33	53 3/8	73.33	73 3/8
18	24.00	24	28.58	28 5/8	32.66	32 5/8	45.00	45	60.00	60	82.50	82 1/2
20	26.67	26 5/8	31.75	31 3/4	36.28	36 1/4	50.00	50	66.67	66 5/8	91.67	91 5/8
22	29.33	29 3/8	34.92	34 7/8	39.91	39 7/8	55.00	55	73.33	73 3/8	100.83	100 7/8
24	32.00	32	38.10	38 1/8	43.54	43 1/2	60.00	60	80.00	80	110	110

Read the O scale lumber size in the first column (available in hobby shops), then move to the columns for your scale: The first gives the scale equivalence in a decimal form, the second in a fractional form to the nearest 1/8 of a scale inch.

Table 6-3. HO Scale Lumber.

HO	O		S		00		TT		N		Z	
1	0.55	1/2	0.73	3/4	0.87	7/8	1.34	1 1/8	1.84	1 7/8	2.53	2 1/2
2	1.10	1 1/8	1.47	1 1/2	1.75	1 3/4	2.76	2 3/4	3.67	3 3/8	5.05	5
3	1.65	1 5/8	2.20	2 1/4	2.62	2 5/8	4.13	4 1/8	5.51	5 1/2	7.58	7 1/2
4	2.20	2 1/4	2.94	3	3.50	3 1/2	5.51	5 1/2	7.35	7 3/8	10.10	10 1/8
6	3.31	3 1/4	4.40	4 3/8	5.24	5 1/4	8.27	8 1/4	11.02	11	15.15	15 1/8
8	4.41	4 3/8	5.87	5 7/8	7.00	7	11.02	11	14.70	14 3/4	20.20	20 1/4
10	5.51	5 1/2	7.34	7 3/8	8.74	8 3/4	13.78	13 3/4	18.37	18 3/8	25.25	25 1/4
12	6.61	6 5/8	8.81	8 7/8	10.49	10 1/2	16.54	16 1/2	22.04	22	30.30	30 1/4
14	7.71	7 3/4	10.28	10 1/4	12.25	12 1/4	19.29	19 1/4	25.72	25 3/4	35.35	35 3/8
16	8.82	8 7/8	11.74	11 3/4	13.98	14	22.05	22	29.39	29 3/8	40.40	40 3/8
18	9.92	9 7/8	13.21	13 1/4	15.73	15 3/4	24.80	24 3/4	33.07	33	45.45	45 1/2
20	11.02	11	14.68	14 3/4	17.48	17 1/2	27.56	27 1/2	36.74	36 3/4	50.50	50 1/2
22	12.12	12 1/8	16.15	16 1/8	19.23	19 1/4	30.32	30 1/4	40.41	40 3/8	55.55	55 1/2
24	13.22	13 1/4	17.62	17 1/8	20.98	21	33.07	33	44.09	44	60.60	60 5/8

Read the HO scale lumber size in the first column (available in hobby shopes), then move to the columns for your scale: The first gives the scale equivalence in a decimal form, the second in fractional form to the nearest 1/8 of a scale inch.

of wood. At times the lumber supply has been sporadic, and having your own stockpile will prevent any disappointments. I generally buy about three times the lumber I need for a model to keep the woodpile filled for those little projects that are fun but don't merit a trip to the hobby shop, or those projects that are inspired when the store is closed.

To store my lumber, I've built a little rack from an old paneling-sample display stand. It holds the various sizes quite well (Fig. 6-2). The upright open design allows me to keep a close watch on the supply, use even short scrap pieces, and reorder when the supply gets low.

If at all possible, I prefer to select my wood in person. Check a few randomly selected pieces at both ends and in the middle with a small ruler, or better yet, an caliper, to see that the cross section is uniform. Beware of wood with very heavy fuzz or saw swirls. These may look innocent but will, no doubt, cause you to spend hours of sanding to remove them from the finished project.

In selecting sheetwood be cautious of large, dark areas or coarse grains that run across the wood. The sheet is actually designed to represent many individual boards ganged together; so a continuous coarse grain that runs directly across the piece destroys the image of individual boards. Sanding between boards is just not the answer. Select the clearest, straightest pieces with the least grain possible.

COLORING WOOD

Stain and paint are the two basic methods for coloring wood. Paint contains a pigment and vehicle that literally covers the wood with a coating of color. Stains, on the other hand, are colored but not opaque, and allow the grain to easily show through.

Many varieties of hobby paints are available; among them, Flouquil is the most common. Most paints have a solvent base, but some, such as Flouquil's Polly S, are water-based. Model paints have finely ground pigments to prevent them from hiding details; so two or three light coats are generally better than one heavy one. As stated earlier, basswood will raise a stiff grain after the first painting. Fine sandpaper can be used to remove this grain before the second coat is applied, and results in a very smooth finish. For rough wood cars or older buildings, the fuzz can actually enhance the "aging" process.

As a general rule, I paint all my wood material before cutting and assembly, especially if more than one color is involved. It's almost impossible to paint a piece of model trimwork a contrasting color after the model has been assembled. You don't want every piece to have exactly the same new-looking color. Many modelers use a pad-wiping method to give different tones and hues. Take a small pad, cloth, or toweling and add a large dab of paint in the middle. Holding the pad between your thumb

Fig. 6-2. This simple wood rack acts as my "lumberyard." Each size of wood has its own place. The crosspieces, or *keepers*, are spaced to allow access to both short and long pieces, thus minimizing waste.

and forefinger, draw the piece of stripwood or stock through the pad while varying the pressure just a bit. As the paint is consumed, the darkness and character of the coloring will change. Try to produce a stock that is similar in color but subtly different. On larger sheets, the pad may be used to wipe across the wood, but always follow the grain—do not wipe crosswise.

A second method for weathering wood is called *dry brushing.* As wood ages, paint flakes and falls away in large chunks. Although there are other techniques, the easiest method of simulating this flaking is to dip a brush in the chosen color then wipe off much of the paint until the bristles are nearly dry. With a sort of scrubbing action, brush the surface trying not to completely cover it. The effect should be one of a blotched, peeled surface.

The method works best with wood that has already been stained a light gray, then dry-brushed with the chosen color, and finally dulled with a second wash of stain. As with most weathering, too little is better than too much.

Stains are more subtle and are used for weathering or aging models. Many different colors are available from Flouquil. The most common stains I use are light or dark flat black. Aging tends to dull all pains and gives unpainted wood a silvery gray tone. Therefore, I liberally wash all my models with at least a dulling coat of gray stain to kill the new look of fresh paint. Commercial weathering agents are available for this purpose, and some people mix their own using alcohol and various dyes.

The same approach should be used in staining as in painting. Prestain each piece a slightly different color before you cut it. By flowing on the stain and blowing just a bit, the solvent will quickly evaporate and leave a layer of dark specks that nicely simulates dust and dirt. This technique can be used at the base of car walls where mud and dirt are likely to splash and collect.

As with all solvent-based materials, be sure to use paints and stains in a well-ventilated area. Your health should be a first priority.

There is another precaution that should be taken in the use of stains. Because stains are largely solvent, they will be quickly absorbed into the wood itself. For stripwood this is no problem, but if you are weathering or aging an entire wall, the chances for warping and buckling are very real. The model must be sufficiently braced to prevent warpage.

To prevent paints from drying out, seal the caps tightly and store them upside down. With solids at the cap, no air can enter, and paints last much longer. No matter what position it is stored in, the pigment will settle. To aid in mixing, I add 10 pieces of medium-sized lead shot pellets or BBs. When the bottle is shaken, the shot helps to mix the pigment.

GLUES, ADHESIVES, AND JOINTS

Generally only one type of glue is used when dealing with wood: white glue. Available from many manufacturers under the names, such as Elmer's, Ambroid, or School Glue, it is an organic material in a water base that forms a polymer when dry and makes a waterproof bond. There are several variations on this basic theme. Carpenter's glue has a little more tack or initial holding power and the ability to be sanded when dry. The less expensive glues tend to tear, curl, or crack when sanded.

In any adhesive the strength is in a thin film of contact rather than in the glue itself. Use a thin coating rather than a large amount and be sure to press pieces together tightly. This technique will minimize glue oozing our of the joint and make a tight joint without gaps. Clamp, press with weights or just hold in place until the glue is fully set—usually a minimum of 20 minutes. You don't have to delay working on your project while waiting for the glue to dry if you get in the habit of doing

several subassemblies or different aspects of the project at the same time. While the glue on one joint is drying, be setting up another, staining more wood, or sanding previously set joints.

At times in modeling, we do cheat and do not follow exact prototype practice. For example, in a prototype, you will seldom find a real *butt joint*, where the end of one board is attached directly to another (Fig. 6-3), since this is structurally very weak. In its place, the prototype builder would use a lap joint or a mortise and tenon—a sort of hole and tooth joint. In modeling, however, we don't need the added strength; so butt joints are very common. The problem then is that the end of the board exposes the open grain of the wood to the cement. Being water-based, white glue is quickly drawn into the wood and away from the joint.

Many modelers just increase the amount of glue. This can be successful, but it usually results in a glue-smeared joint. To avoid this problem, I use a two-step approach. After cutting the wood to size and checking for proper fit, I apply a liberal coating of glue to the end of the board and allow it to be drawn into the grain and to dry, actually sealing the wood end. Then I apply a second light coating, and the two pieces of wood are joined and clamped until dry. The result is a strong, clean joint. Remember that this double gluing method is only necessary for butt joints.

Although the butt joint is frequently used in model construction, in some cases a slight modification will provide for a better joint. It may be difficult to cut a trim piece to the exact dimension and have it be perfectly square at the same time. Many times it ends up a little too long or just a shade too short, leaving an obvious gap. In those cases, where strength is not important, such as a laminated piece of trim over a scribed sheetwood base, the wood may be cut at a slight angle away from the joint (Fig. 6-4). This is a much more forgiving joint without actually making that "perfect cut."

Glues and adhesives come in many different forms and compositions, but remember, it's not the glue that makes the joint. It's the union of each side of the joint by a film of adhesive. The general rule if that the best joints are those with a large contact

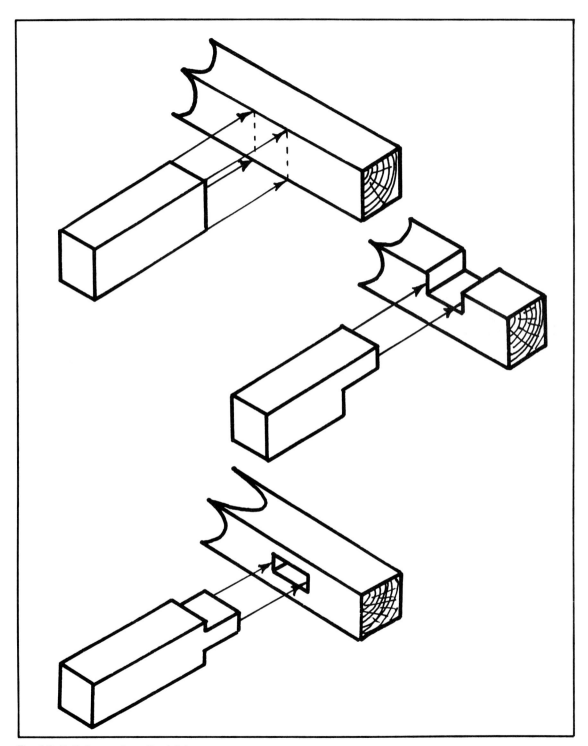

Fig. 6-3. Butt, lap, and mortise joints.

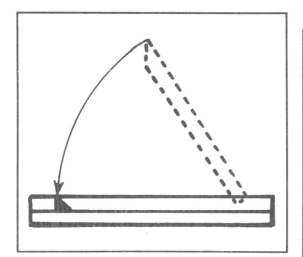

Fig. 6-4. Press fit joint.

Table 6-4. Suggested Glue Usage.

	Wood	Paper	Plastic	Glass	Metal	Plaster
White Glue	E	G	P	P	P	E
Epoxy	G	G	G	E	E	G
ACC*	P	P	E	E	E	P
Contact Cement	E	E	G	E	E	P
Plastic Cement (Thick)	P	E	E	P	P	G
Plastic Liquid Glues (Thin)	P	P	E	P	P	P

E = Excellent
G = Good
P = Poor

* Alpha Cyanoacrylates or "Super Glues" Some newer formulations may be usable with wood.

area, high pressure while setting, and a minimum of glue.

For model work, most glue applicators are crude and oversized. Even when only a small hole is made in the top of a glue bottle, it tends to dry and clog, and there will be times when a good dab of glue will be necessary. I've completely given up on special glue guns and applicators with pins in the tips. Instead I have found the best and easiest method for me is to rescue the flexible plastic lid of a margarine or whipped topping tub from the trash and use it as a glue receptacle. Most glues (including some expoxies) will not adhere to the plastic surface. It's an easy task to squeeze out a dollop of glue into the plastic top, then use a pin, small nail, toothpick, or scrap piece of wood to apply the glue. The more adhesive needed, the larger the applicator needed.

I like to run a bead of glue down the edge of the piece to be attached, then spread it into a thin film with my finger. There should be enough glue to just spread and make contact but not ooze from the joint. Be careful with the fast-acting super glues, since they will almost instantly glue your finger to the work piece as well. Once the unused glue has dried, the solid mass can easily be removed from the plastic top by flexing. Table 6-4 gives a general idea of what types of adhesives to use with different materials.

CUTTING TECHNIQUES

A knife itself may be used to mark the wood for the cut. The cutting action should be with a downward slice rather than a straight push. When cutting a large piece of sheetwood, the cut should be made with several repetitive cuts, going over the same line. Cutting a 1/16-inch thick piece of sheetwood will take 8 to 12 strokes.

Always use a metal straightedge when cutting

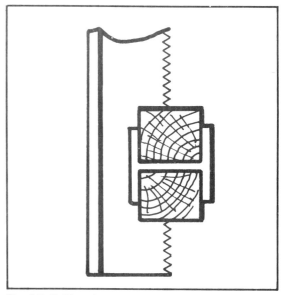

Fig. 6-5. Cutting shapes.

a modeling material. Your hand is simply not steady enough to make a realistically straight line of any length. If at all possible, position the ruler to cover the piece of material you want to save. In this way if the knife slips, it will cut into the excess or scrap and not damage your good piece. The special shapes, such as I-beams, will split if cutting pressure is applied. These should be filled with scrap wood as supports and the entire sandwich cut through (Fig. 6-5). Always keep a sharp cutting edge by replacing blades frequently.

LAYOUT AND CONSTRUCTION

To help eliminate frustration in cutting sides for various cars, use one side as a pattern for another. For example, if you have one side of a caboose cut to size and window openings cut out, it is easier to use the first side as a pattern for the second. Simply place the materials back to back, trace, and cut. Copying one wall from the other will ensure that they are identical mirror images—maybe not a perfect copy of the plans, but identical nevertheless.

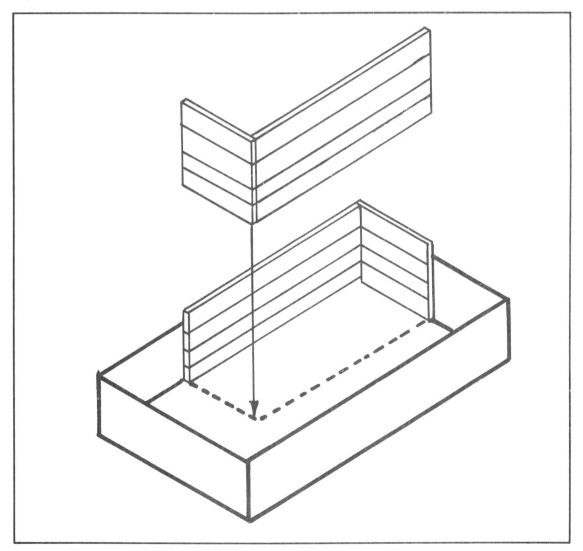

Fig. 6-6. Assembly.

Your goal is for a model that looks perfect if it cannot actually be perfect.

Most wooden cars are made from a boxlike shell with sheetwood walls and solid blocks of wood for end support. Many modelers build up the walls to near completion before assembling it into a box, since it's easier to work with a flat wall on the workbench until it is completely finished. The final assembly must be square and perpendicular to the base. If you assemble the walls sequentially in a kind of circle, it's quite possible that small errors in alignment will keep adding together so your last

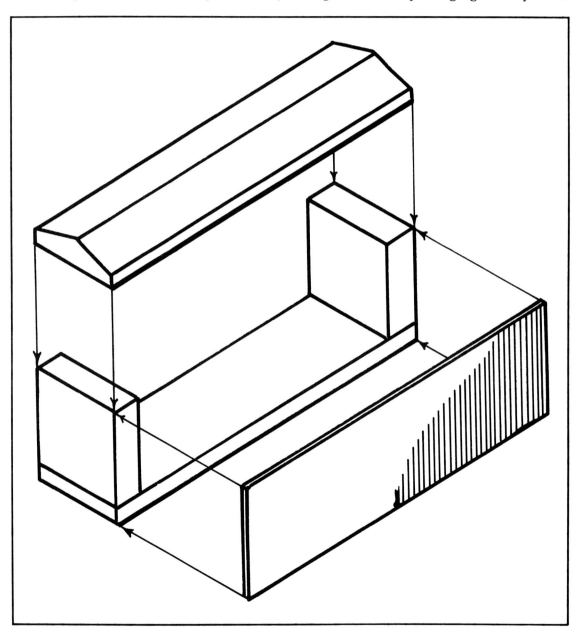

Fig. 6-7. Box construction.

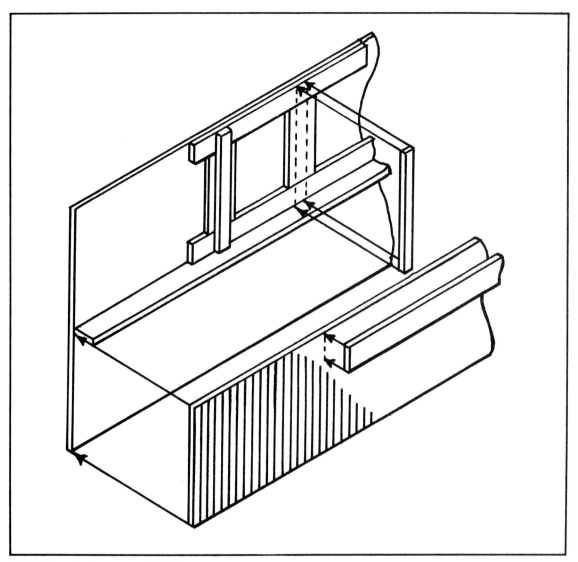

Fig. 6-8. Lamination over a clear base.

joint will be grossly out of line.

For open cars such as gondolas, hoppers, and flat cars, it's best to complete the sides and ends. Then assemble them in two sets (one side and one end) to form *L*. Check that these are square and true. When they are fully dry, assemble the two *L*s into the final body and add the underframe (Fig. 6-6).

Closed cars like boxcars or refrigerator cars, where interiors do not show, are frequently made

using a solid wood base and thick blocks for ends. An overlay of scribed wood finished the model (Fig. 6-7).

If you are planning a very elaborate model, like a fully detailed passenger car, a technique called *lamination* can be used. Real cars have either a wood or steel interior framing, but this is seldom modeled. Instead a solid sheet of wood or plastic forms a base, and both the interior and exterior walls are built up on it in layers. If you are using

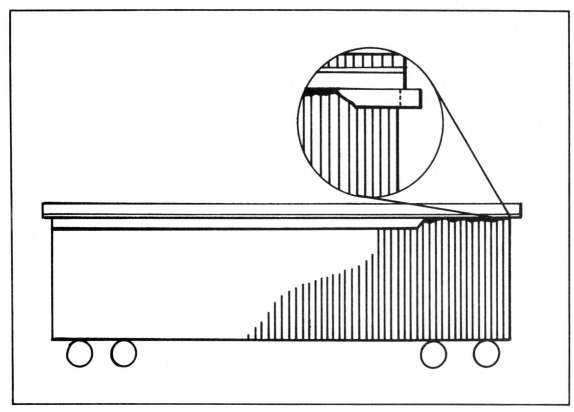

Fig. 6-9. Fascia hides errors.

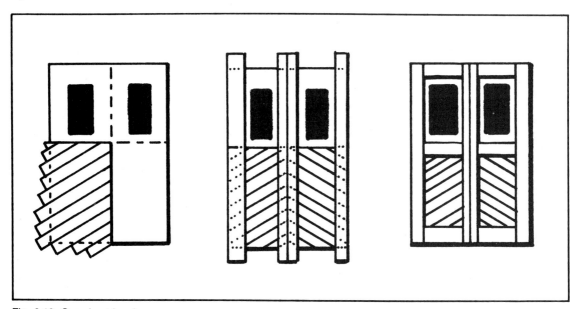

Fig. 6-10. Oversize trimmings.

64

plastic, the base can be 0.010 or 0.020 clear styrene for the entire wall, with prepainted strips and sheets laminated over it to cover all but the window opening (Fig. 6-8). Lamination may take a little planning on your part, but it is worth the effort.

You can also use partial lamination to hide mistakes or poor joints. No one is perfect, and it is very seldom that parts match exactly. Use of trim can hide many errors. For example, on a car side, the bottom of the side should be made exactly square and flat; the use of the trim or fascia at the top is to cover any imperfection (Fig. 6-9). Door and window trim on passenger cars should also be added later to hide errors.

Another hint is to measure and cut your pieces directly from the model rather than indirectly from the plans. For example, a piece like a chair rail or door trim should be left oversize by 1/8 inch or so, then trimmed back to a perfect fit when the model is assembled (Fig. 6-10). Be careful trimming off these small extensions; use a very sharp knife and place a scrap piece of wood behind the item being cut. It takes a great deal of force, which might break off an unsupported detail.

That's about it for ideas. Now let's do some building in wood.

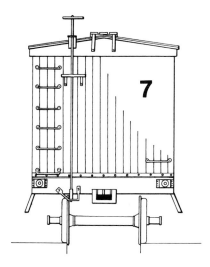

Freight Cars

T HE JOB OF CARRYING FREIGHT TO ALL COR-
ners of the country required the railroads to
develop many different types of cars through the
years. In a very similar progression to that of the
passenger car, the earliest freight cars were no
more than wagons on steel wheels, although early
on there were specialized cars. During the Civil
War, cannon batteries were carried on flat cars and
moved to the front whenever possible. But from the
1860s well into the 1920s, the basic design of the
freight car was the 36-to 40-foot sheathed boxcar.
During World War I, the United States Railroad
Administration (USRA) standardized the design for
freight cars to be built during the war. Since handling freight was such a basic type of operation, the
design changed little over the years.

VARIATIONS

There were two general styles. Single sheathed
cars had horizontal planking on the inside of a metal
framework. (Fig. 7-1) These cars can occasionally

be seen even today in work trains. Recently, I
stumbled across a string on the Soo Line in suburban Chicago marked "EXPLOSIVES . . . do not
hump." Now I don't know if there really were any
explosives in them, but I stayed clear.

The second style of car was the double-
sheathed car, which had horizontal wood sheathing
on the inside and vertical small board sheathing on
the outside. Many of these cars were used for hauling grain in loose form by adding a small barrier
(grain door) inside the regular door to keep the load
from spilling out. Of course these were in the days
when other commodities didn't contaminate the car,
although you might have found some coal mixed
in with the grain if you were not careful.

Add insulation in the walls, waterproof the inside, and you have a refrigerator car. Today each
car carries a power-generating engine and refrigeration system, but not that long ago the fruit ex-
presses from the south had to be iced and reiced
on their trips to the north. Many railroads around
the large cities carried on thriving businesses cut-

Fig. 7-1. An outside braced boxer has one layer of sheathing running horizontally with metal bracing on the exterior.

ting ice from the lakes and rivers in the winters, storing it in ice houses and delivering the cold blocks to the city during the summer. All this handling required special refrigerator cars that could insulate the ice during shipment. Refrigerator cars are easily recognized by the small, very thick doors (Fig.7-2).

Of course it was possible for things to get too

Fig. 7-2. Refrigerator cars can be recognized by the small doors in heavily insulated walls. Old cars would have ice hatches on the roof corners, while more modern cars have ventilated sides for the compressor engines.

cold for the produce and to have the lettuce and carrots freeze solid on their trips north. The answers were a whole series of patented heating units and ventilator systems that scooped air into the cars, heated it over charcoal, alcohol, and oil fires and circulated the warm air through the cars. Although seldom modeled, a little searching in the library or through some of the old car builders cyclopedias may get you very interesting detail to add to your model cars.

Car decorations on the refrigerators and boxcars ranged form simple to flamboyant. At one time the "billboard reefers" hawked their contents of milk, pickles, beer, or cheese with huge, colorful signs across the sides of the cars. The NMRA annually publishes color car sides in all the popular scales of some of these delightful cars. The high cost of upkeep and changes in ICC rules lead to their demise.

In the basic box design are also the bulk haulers—the hoppers and gondolas. The very early bulk cars were simply flat cars with sides added, and the coal or rocks had to be shoveled in and out. Improvement on the design included cars with draglines and blades resembling snowplows that pushed through the car dumping the material out of the ends. The obvious design change was to make the car bottoms tipped and allow the materials to flow out the bottom through hopper doors. The original cars were wood, but steel very quickly began to replace it. As early as 1905, pressed steel cars made from metal sheets and folded metal angles riveted together began to appear (Fig. 7-3). These cars could be modeled in styrene with excellent results. During World War II because of metal shortages, the hoppers had a composite design-wood with a metal frame. The Norfolk and Western had a series of beautiful 100-ton wood coal hoppers.

A set of early steel cars originally made for the

Fig. 7-3. High in the White Mountains of Arizona, this riveted ore car built in 1905 continued to serve the the Apache Railroad until the middle 1970's. It would make a good paper or plastic project with embossed rivets.

Fig. 7-4. On this Quincy Mining Co. ore car, the side, center, and intermediate sills are easily recognized as they join with a very massive end sill.

Great Northern found its way to the Yosemite Valley Railroad in the 40s for gypsum hauling and to the Apache Railroad for copper mining. I photographed a string in 1971 that was still in service.

Of course there were, and are, many variations for special uses—cattle cars, metal coil cars, tank cars, depressed center flat cars, coke cars, the list goes on. Some were especially designed for particular loads, like the express cars that ran in the "silk trains." Exceptionally valuable trains of raw silk were received on the West Coast and raced across country to the garment manufacturing centers in the East. These cargoes were so valuable that special locked vaults were located at freight yards where entire cars were stored under lock and key.

TERMS

Since most of the hardware terms have not changed through the years, let's take a close look at an older car and then consider the changes that have taken place to give us the modern railroad car.

The frame of most wooden cars consisted of a sturdy timber box. Each timber in the base was called a *sill*, with long center, side, and intermediate sills forming the framing pieces, and short but heavy end sills to close the box (Fig. 7-4). Frequently these sills were of very heavy and unusually sized lumber, like 5 × 9 or 9 × 7. When you are measuring actual railroad drawings, you may find these dimensions (your scale rule is not wrong). For a while these sizes were available in model lumber, but the supplier is now out of business. I did follow one of my cardinal rules and bought three times what I needed. Keep your eyes open; the supply may return.

If you can't find the exact scale lumber you need, try a substitution with the closest size. The frames were usually joined with mortise-and-tenon joints, often with a pin through the joint. Going across the car near the middle were two or more crossbraces, called *needle beams*. Positioned on the needle beams were metal posts or brackets, called *queen posts* Fig. 7-5. As the car loading increased, there was a tendency for the car floor to buckle and sometimes cave in. To counter this force, long rods were run from the end sills under the car, over the queen posts, and finally out the other end sill. These were the *truss rods* and could be tightened both by turn buckles in the middle and nuts on the ends. The expression "riding the rods" comes from the hobo habit of climbing onto the trussrods under a freight car and going for a free ride. Some modelers use fine wire for truss rods, while I prefer to use light nylon fishline that can be drawn tight over the queen posts. When tied off at both ends, the line can be lifted up onto the queen posts, stretching it to a tight fit. If you have chosen the line correctly, it can also be strung through the turn buckle castings. Paint the line a grimy black but don't paint the part that runs through the turnbuckle. The fishline will actually look like two separate rods meeting at the turnbuckle. On the prototype, the turnbuckle is threaded in such a way so when turned it pulls the rods into the center from both directions.

Added at the car bottom are two sloping platforms which accept the trucks. They are called *body bolsters* and might be wood, metal, or a combination (Fig. 1-6). Some had small outrigger type bearing surfaces to steady the car on the truck as it rocked along the track.

The body of a boxcar, also called a *house car*, was made from a second wood box mounted onto

Fig. 7-5. The large truss rods on this old car pass down and under the metal queen post castings that rest on the crossing needle beam.

Fig. 7-6. You don't see the bottom of a car very often, but this overturned gondola shows a metal plate bolster.

the underframe. The wooden posts that make up the wall are held to the floor by small metal castings called post, end, door, and corner *pockets*. The walls are grooved siding, called *sheathing*, that usually runs parallel to the underframe. Some cars are single-sheathed; others double-sheathed with both an exterior and interior wall, depending on the cargo they would normally haul. Of course special cars like refrigerators would have extra insulation, and special waterproof covering plus extra doors, vents, and special hardware.

On the prototype, the roof is shaped by either a series of wooden forms or metal castings, called *carlines*. They are formed to the pitch of the roof and have notches for long pieces, called *purlins* (Fig. 7-7). The roof proper is laid over the purlins and terminate at the very top beam of the roof, which is the *ridgepole*. Trimming the roof at the top are the side and end fascia strips, or boards. They make

a tight seal between the sheathing and the roof itself. The roof is crowned with running boards, also called a *roof walk*, which allows trainmen to move from car to car and hand-activate brakes where necessary. Many small *grab irons*, or hand railings, appear in strategic places about the car.

The braking system represents the last, and perhaps most complex, part of each car. Using a system of floating levers, bars, and fulcrums, pressure from the air reservoir is uniformly transmitted to brake shoes on each of the truck wheels. The signal for the brakes to be applied and to what degree is received along the train pipeline and controlled by a triple valve on the brake cylinder of each car. If the train line is accidently broken, the brakes automatically apply. Runaways result if the pressure in the reservoir is not sufficient to clamp the brakes hard enough to hold the train. Older cars generally use a K-type brake

Fig. 7-7. This rare photo of the interior of a double-sheathed wood boxcar shows wooden carlines forming the roof contour. The top vertical beam is the ridge pole, while the lighter beams running the length of the car roof are called purlins. On more modern cars, the wooden carlines were replaced with metal formers.

system, which normally has a single unit for the valve, cylinder, and reservoir. Modern air brakes are called AB types, with separate valves, cylinders, and reserve tanks.

Very few modelers reproduce entire brake systems, except for the highest quality contest models. One of the problems is that the brake levers and rods must be connected to trucks, which severely restrict their turning motion and cause many derailments. Modelers frequently mount a good casting of a brake cylinder in an obvious place under the car, add a few pieces of wire for lines and levers, and leave it at that. I've followed that route a number of times, and it is seemingly sufficient. Working brakes are beyond the scope of this book, but they are explained in most of the car builders cyclopedias. Build as much as you feel comfortable with doing.

Couplers haven't changed much in design of the locking system, although at one time there were dozens of types before standardization. What was changed is the *draft gear*, or the cushioning mechanism which connects the coupler to the car. A very early type of coupler was the *link and pin*, which has no more than a simple chain between cars. As the train begins to move, however, each car receives a jerk as the "slack is taken out." With a long, modern train, this jerking motion intensifies until couplers can be pulled completely out, to say nothing of shaking up the crew in the caboose.

To minimize the damage, the draft gear have been designed with more resilience. Complex spring and bar arrangement absorb much of the shock, creating a much longer draft gear, which tends to stick out the end of the car. Sometimes the coupler sticks in the retracted position, and when an unsuspecting worker or railfan touches it, it springs out with a terrible punch.

CHANGE IN DESIGN

In more modern cars, it was not so much a change in design but a gradual modification of materials and manufacturing processing. The first changes were the introduction of metal parts to repair and replace wooden ones. A whole series of companies around 1920 began making metal roofs and ends to replace the aging and damaged wood ones. The primary design change was to use pressed or corrugated metal. The new ends came in horizontal forms—the familiar dreadnaught end—in vertical ribbing, and even some that had corrugation in complete circles, such as the Bull's Eye end of the Cleveland Car Company. Roofs also came in plates, pressed parts, and even corrugations similar to the barn-type roofing.

Construction was slowly coming toward all metal. The various sills were replaced, first by cast metal center sills and intermediate sills, and finally by welded and fabricated underbodies that could be much larger, yet lighter and stronger. Gone were the queen posts and trussrods. The sides no longer needed posts and wood sheathing, but could be made larger without increases in weight. The concept of corrugation for strength continued and can be seen in many modern cars, including those with "waffle" sides, which is just another form of corrugation. Doors have become much larger to accommodate the large variety of materials being shipped. The C&NW through Marengo, Illinois ships hundreds of "Hi-Cube" cars-very large boxcars of bulky auto parts to the assembly plant in a nearby town. A welded metal underframe makes possible what a wood structure just could not support (Fig. 7-8).

Changing times have dictated the creation and loss of some styles of cars. Changes in the methods of meat processing have eliminated the need for cattle cars, while the shipping of bulk chemicals, fer-

Fig. 7-8. Changes in government tax incentives and per diem charges has brought abut a rash of investments in short line and specialty railroad cars. This modern boxcar has short ladders, a corrugated roof, and no roof walk.

Fig. 7-9. Seldom seen in revenue service, a stock car would make an excellent model in wood or styrene. Wayne examines this one at the Illinois Railway Museum in Union, Illinois.

tilizers, and food have brought on the development of giant air-slide hoppers with complete covers to protect the lading from the weather (Fig. 7-9).

Gone on the new cars are roof walks. Since the late 1960s, these walks were no longer required because labor rules eliminated the hazardous job of running along the top of cars to set brakes on individual cars. Locomotive and train braking were considered sufficient to control most operations.

There are a few books on prototype freight cars, such as the *Car Builders Cyclopedia* (Simmons-Boardman) published every four years and available to modelers at better hobby shops. Researching the strange and unusual cars of the 1920's can be a real treasure hunt; building the modern high-capacity cars can be real fun. Try your hand at both.

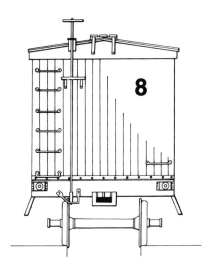

Building a Kitbashed Work Car

MANY PEOPLE FEEL THAT THE ERA OF wooden cars ended in the 1920s following World War I when metals were released from the war effort and could be used for domestic railroad cars. (There actually was a Chicago Concrete Car Company that manufactured gondolas and flat cars from reinforced concrete because of the metal shortages.) The active production of wooden cars does date from the beginning of the railroad industry until about the 1920s when all steel cars began to appear with regularity. In truth, wooden cars survive even until today, primarily in nonrevenue service for track work or even deprived of their trucks as stationary storage facilities off along some weed-grown siding. This first project was found on the Burlington Northern in 1982. So if you are inclined to try kitbashing or scratchbuilding a wood project, don't let the fact that your railroad is from a more modern era bother you. For the wood projects in this book, I've tried to provide a mixture of kit modifications that could be used in any time period and some purely older cars a 1920s fan would just love. Don't feel shy about trying any or all of them.

It may be a lot of fun to put a kit together for any particular model, but there is the problem that the finished product is not really special. Hundreds, perhaps thousands, of other modelers have the same model. More importantly, it may not be exactly what you want for a given scene on your railroad. Scratchbuilding may be too difficult or take too long; so a good solution is *kitbashing*— taking a commercial kit or even finished model and modifying it to meet your needs. The modification may be just a few new parts and a coat of paint or a complete rebuilding, but the finished product can be the highlight of a layout scene.

For this project in wooden kitbashing, I've picked one of my favorite prototype models— maintenance of the way equipment. There are thousands of freight cars on a typical railroad, but only a handful of maintenance cars. For years the repair work on railroads was done by nomadic groups of strong men who worked on the track crews and were housed right along the right-of-way

Fig. 8-1. The prototype for our model is an old work car, probably built in the 1920's and surviving to at least 1982 when this photo was taken at Mendota, Illinois.

Fig. 8-2. Although battered, there is a wooden step running at the truss-rod level under both the personnel and freight doors. Notice the metal strap along the bottom of the car and the clear rows of nail marks.

Fig. 8-3. The freight door is really battered, but it is clearly made of two thicknesses of wood running perpendicular to each other.

in crew cars. For work far from towns and cities, the work train would not only include bunk cars and cook cars, but hospital, payroll, and training facilities. These crew trains were really traveling towns. Today crews stay closer to home. Although some railroads designed and built the crew facilities from scratch, it was more likely that they would rebuild some of their older retired revenue cars. The old wood boxcars kept serving as work cars. Actually it was a kind of prototype kitbashing, where

Fig. 8-4. The end is a metal replacement part that comes in two pieces.

a car intended for one purpose was rebuilt for a completely different one.

Currently crews do not travel away from home as often, and with the demise of the passenger train a large number of more luxurious passenger cars have become available for crew service. Some of the wooden cars are still to be found, and I was lucky enough to photograph this car on the Burlington Northern at Mendota, Illinois in 1982. It's a simple double-sheathed boxcar, with doors and windows added for the work service.

I began looking for a kit to convert by searching back through my collection of unbuilt kits. All modelers seem to stockpile kits, but I guess that's only part of the hobby. There were several possibilities, but I honestly felt I didn't want to "waste" a good kit in case I messed it up. So I wandered over to the junk pile—modelers also

never throw anything away—and found an unfinished wooden boxcar I had messed up in cutting a few parts. Now was a chance to build a new model, as well as use an unwanted kit. I have no prototype information about this project except for the photos. The conversion is quite simple and includes putting in several windows and two personnel doors and replacing the wooden ends with pressed metal ends and a metal roof. I suspect the original car had a wooden roof and ends which were upgraded by the railroad with metal ends.

I'll try to work through the conversion so you can follow with a similar kit or built-up car of your own. Follow both the directions and Figs. 8-1 through 8-23.

☐ The kit was assembled with the walls, ends, and roof, but not the doors or roof walk. For the windows, I used commercial plastic castings, while the ends were metal parts salvaged from another kit. Commercial castings are also available for these parts. I had to move the window openings back a little from the ends to clear the wooden end blocks that are inside the car. It didn't bother me at all because this is my kitbashing project. The door is from a passenger part set, but many other windows and doors could be substituted.

☐ To give the car a little extra flair, I threw out the standard wooden door and built one up from a sheet of scribed wood with grooves running

Fig. 8-5. At the corners many details can be seen, such as the metal corner and side plates, the many nuts and bolts, and the diagonal rods running down into the sides of the car. For the super detailers in the crowd, this photograph could produce many hours of fun.

Fig. 8-6. The back side is the reverse of the front, with the exception of the boxlike piece under the windows. I'm not sure of its function.

Fig. 8-7. Construction begins with a partially assembled wooden boxcar kit. The plastic castings to be used are in front of the model.

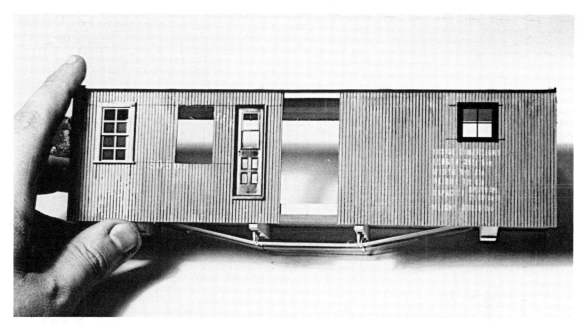

Fig. 8-8. The positions for the doors and windows are measured directly on the model. The windows had to be moved in a little from the ends to clear the large wooden blocks inside which make up the car body. Use a sharp, hard pencil to mark the model. Pen or magic marker have ink that will bleed through the future layers of paint.

Fig. 8-9. The metal ends were salvaged from another kit, but ends can be purchased from large manufacturers.

Fig. 8-10. The top fascia at the ends is cut by repeated trimming with an X-acto knife so it fits in place.

Fig. 8-11. To simulate the weathered door, a piece of horizontally scribed wood was used as the base, with individual 1-x-3 pieces glued on in the opposite direction. Break a few and rough up a few with a razor saw or very coarse sandpaper. Try to stain or paint the pieces slightly different colors.

Fig. 8-12. The door is glued in place and held with a heavy weight. Smaller roof fascia is clamped in place with clothespins.

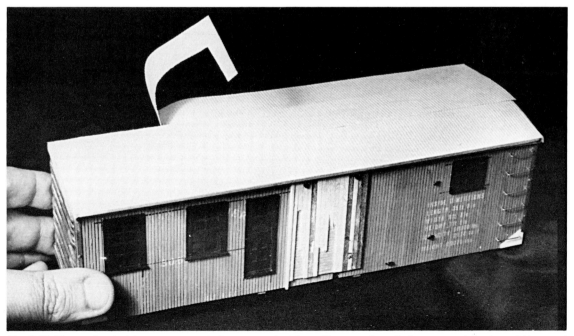

Fig. 8-13. The roof material was a corrugated paper product from Simpson. Campbell corrugated stock would be used as well, or just a flat metal roof simulated with paper or plastic.

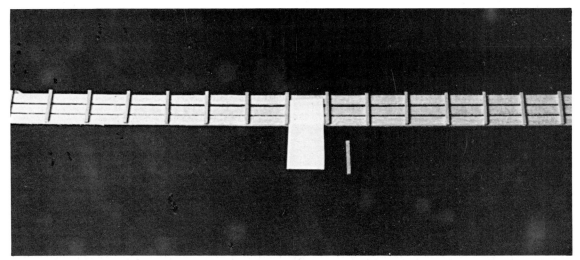

Fig. 8-14. The roof walk was assembled separately from 1-1/2- x -6 pieces glued to 2- x -2 supports. A small piece of plastic was used as a spacer to ensure all the supports were equally spaced.

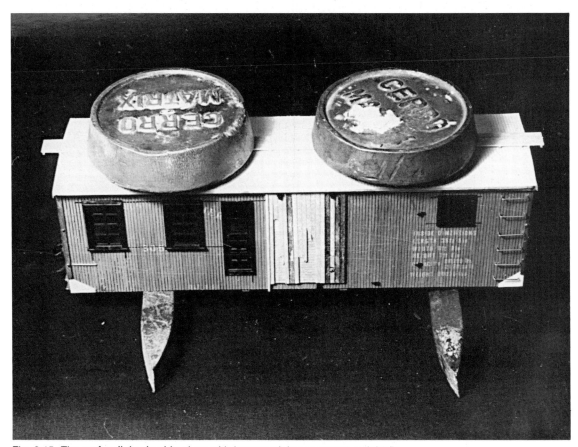

Fig. 8-15. The roof walk is glued in place with heavy weights to ensure a tight fit.

Fig. 8-16. The entire car was sprayed with Maintenance-of-way orange then dusted with a soft cosmetic brush and dry, powdered tempera color. The color I like is an earth tone called *seal brown*, but many others would be acceptable. Consider your type of terrain—yellow clay, red oxides, black minerals etc.

Figs. 8-17 and 8-18. Two views of the finished model show that a simple boxcar kit can be easily modified into an interesting piece of rolling stock that's unique to your railroad.

Fig. 8-19. The door has a nice two-step stairway. Notice the wire gates over the windows.

horizontally and a lot of small pieces of 1 × 3 glued on vertically. Some of the ends were broken and twisted; so the door looks really damaged and aged. The door was glued on against a 3- × -3 stop with Grandt cast hardware.

☐ Depending on the kit you start with, it may be necessary to complete a fascia or trim around the roof and at the ends. I used green model airplane putty to fill in any cracks and to smooth over mistakes.

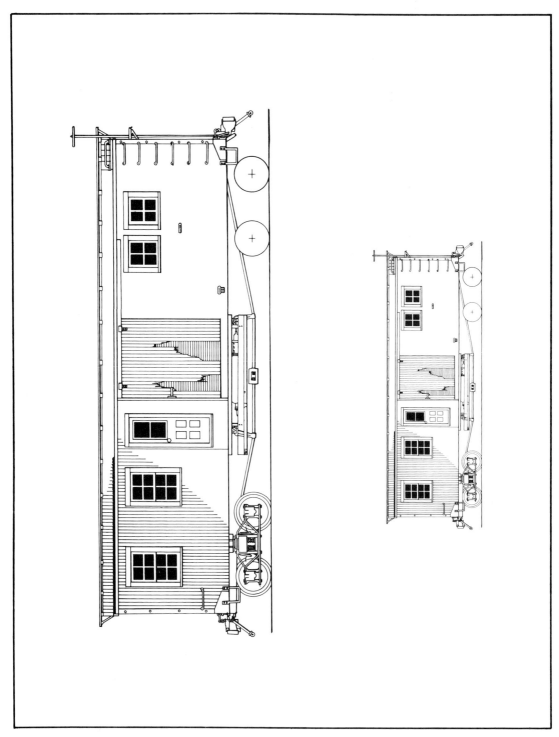

Fig. 8-20. Side view of the kitbashed work car (HO and N scales).

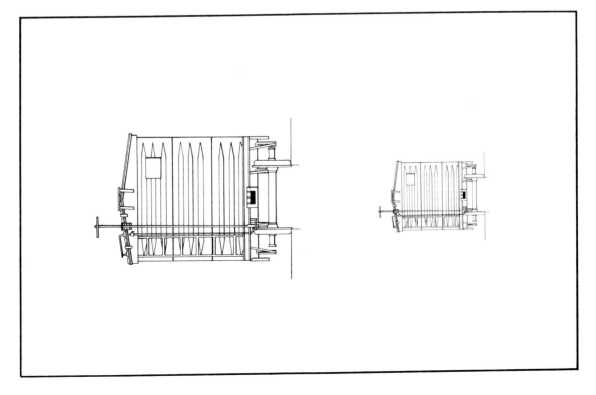

Fig. 8-21. Rear view of the kitbashed work car (HO and N scales).

Fig. 8-22. If you would like to try kitbashing another work car, try this one. It was photographed on the Chicago and Northwestern in West Chicago, Illinois about 1950. Begin by purchasing an outside-braced wooden car. With all the windows, this could be a bunk car.

☐ One of the first things to go on an old wood car was the roof. In the 1920s and 1930s, many manufacturers began producing a pressed metal replacement roof that would fit over the wood base. One of these manufacturers was the Sharon Steel Company of Sharon, Ohio, which made a simple corrugated roof. I used a corrugated paper material for my roof, but several manufacturers make pressed metal material that works as well. A spray adhesive was used to fix the roof to the car.

☐ The roof walk is three pieces of 1 1/2 × 6 with 2-×-2 supports. The roof walk was prepared separately before being attached to the roof. Add any additional detail you may see in the photos or some special ones of your own.

☐ The entire car—top, sides, and bottom—is painted with a maintenance-of-way orange. The car, however, needs a little bit of aging and some highlighting. I washed the entire car with a very dilute mix of black leather dye (not shoe polish) in rubbing (isopropyl) alcohol. Brush some along the top and bottom of the sides, allowing the stain to run up the grooves in the wood. Be careful on the roof if you are using a paper corrugated material, because the alcohol may cause it to warp. When the weathering is dark enough and dirty enough to suit you, allow it to fully dry. The car still seemed a little too bright for me; so I dusted it with very light brown powdered tempera paint. Powdered chalk could be used as well.

The finished model has a real working man's look and should be a nice addition to your layout. I've also included photos for another work car with lots of windows and vents, which could be the basis

Fig. 8-23. The end has only a minor modification with a small door to walk from car to car. With all the bracing on the outside of the car, it will be a matter of fitting the doors and windows between the braces. This could really be a fun project.

for your own kitbashing project. The prototype is a Chicago & Northwestern car photographed at West Chicago, Illinois about 1950. A simple out- side braced kit could be used with the windows located between the bracing. Kitbashing can be fun. Try it!

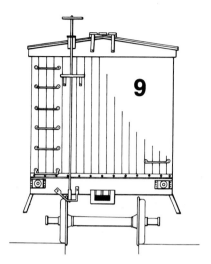

Building an
Air-Operated Rail Loader

I'M AFRAID THE DAYS OF THE HE-MEN ARE over. We need a sky cap at the airport, a red cap at the hotel, and a carry-out boy at the supermarket. There was a time, though, when real manual labor was the only way that things were done. The track gangs of the railroads even in the early 1900s did things very much by hand. The automated, all-in-one track machine was yet to be invented. So for a first project in wood I'd like to look at those times with an Air Rail Loader (and unloader) designed by G.D. Brooke, division engineer of the Baltimore and Ohio Railroad and reported in a 1920 *Railway Age Gazette.*

Rail was provided in 33-foot lengths that weighed up to 150 pounds per yard and more for the "high iron." Lifting and positioning these heavy sections was a job requiring an entire crew of men with rail tongs working in unison, often to the cadence of the gandy dancers' foreman. Since repairs were done in many places and rail was only occasionally used, the permanent commitment of a large mobile crane to a small work crew was in-

appropriate. Instead this little doubled-ended loader was developed. Powered by compressed air from the locomotive along the normal train line, the designers claimed "Seven men to a boom are required to work the loader to it's capacity. Once such gang will load or unload as much rail in a day as a gang of twenty men throwing it on or off the cars." Robotics had reached the 20th century, and men were replaced by machines!

Actually the loader has two identical ends with frames and hoists at each end. The boom extends over a flatcar or gondola loaded with rail, and the hoist lifts the rail up. Workmen then push it over the side as the 3/4-inch wire rope is lowering the rail. The boom does not swing from side to side, as with more elaborate rail cranes.

I chose to model the crane with only one end operable and the extra boom stored on the car. Actually it's the kind of item that might be found in the weeds behind an old roundhouse well into the 1940s or 1950s. It's a good beginning project for someone just starting to work with wood. None of

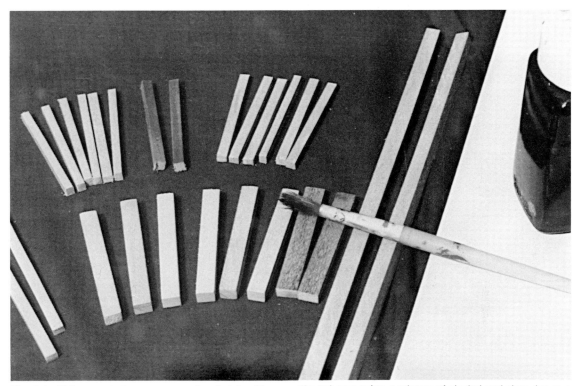

Fig. 9-1. All the wood pieces are precut and stained to a weathered gray using a mixture of alcohol and shoe dye or a commercial stain.

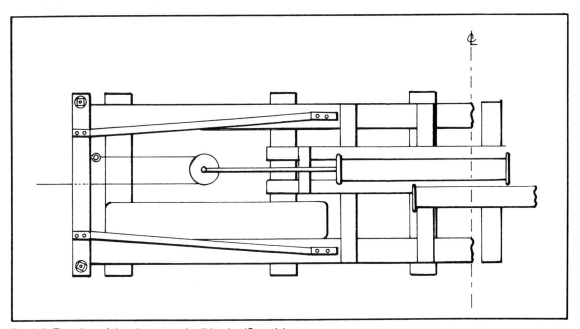

Fig. 9-2. Top view of the air-operated rail loader (O scale).

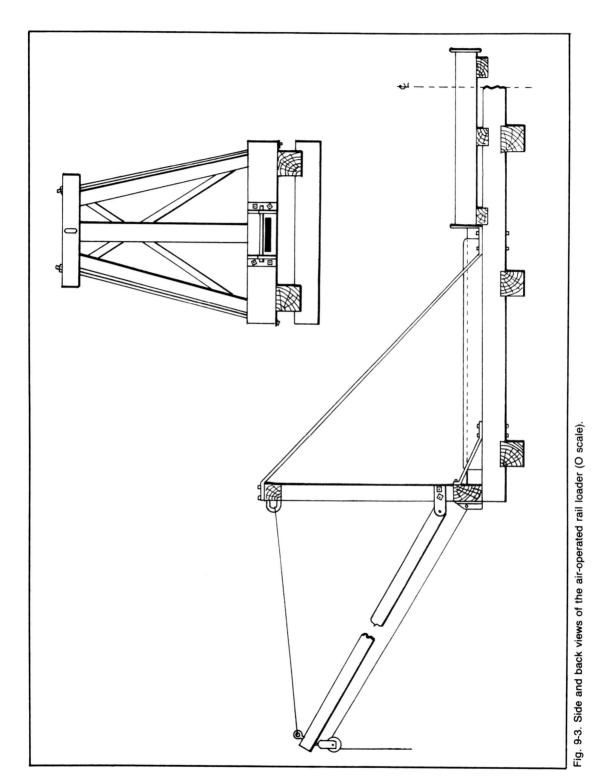

Fig. 9-3. Side and back views of the air-operated rail loader (O scale).

the dimensions are critical, and the results will be a nice model to put up front for visitors to see.

Begin by selecting the basic lumber for the car from clear basswood. Stain all the pieces a weathered black, using a mix of alcohol and black dye or old brush cleanings if you save the used solvent,or one of the commercial weathering agents. Be sure to do this before you cut or begin to glue the model together. Many glues will not take stain, and it's very difficult to cover the glue spots that inevitably occur.

☐ Cut and stain the following set of material see Figs. 9-1 through 9-3.

two 10" × 12" × 32'
two 10" × 12" × 8'
two 8" × 14" × 8'
two 6" × 8" × 24'
two 8" × 8" × 4'8"

two 8" × 8" × 8'
ten 6" × 8" × 8'

☐ The main frame is constructed by building a boxlike structure using the 32-foot 10 × 12s as the side sills and crossing them with the 6 pieces of 8-foot-×-10-inch-×-12-inch stringers set in notches. The first little hint is a method of getting those notches to line up exactly on both long pieces. Hold, or better yet clamp, the long pieces together, and cut the notches in both pieces at the same time (Fig. 9-4). Begin at each end, following the plans and equally space the grooves toward the middle, to prevent small errors from building up as you go across and having the last cut badly out of place. Using a saw, cut into each side, then slice out the excesses with a razor, and finally finish with a flat file.

☐ Glue the base unit together with white glue

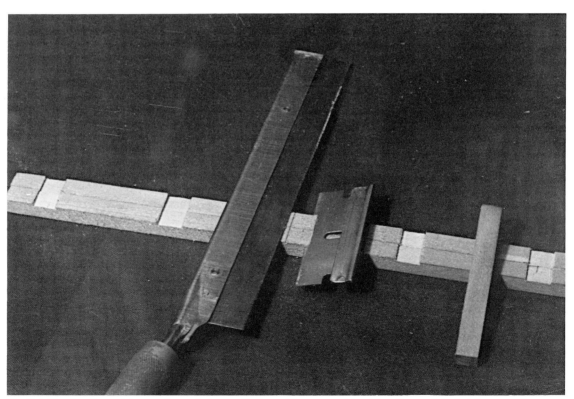

Fig. 9-4. To align the notches on the main beam, the two stringers are joined together, notched at the same time, and then separated.

using a 4 and 1/2-foot spacer between the long beams to keep them at exactly the same seperation all along the car. Again put on the end pieces first and work toward the middle. Keep checking with a square to see that the unit is true. Once the two end pieces are dry, add the intermediate ones, pushing the entire unit against a straightedge or block to ensure that all the pieces extend beyond the frame to the same amount (Fig. 9-5). Use weights to hold the cross pieces in place while the glue sets, then sand the bottom of the finished unit by slowly swirling it over a piece of fine sandpaper on a flat surface like a sheet of glass. This last step should not be omitted, since it will prevent the unit from wobbling once it is placed in a car body.

□ The two derricks come next. The base is the 8-×-14-inch piece, the top 8-×-8-inches × 4 feet 8 inches, and the uprights 6 × 8 inches on sides 8 × 8 inches in the middle. Put the center piece in first, then fit the other two in place, slanting them as needed (Fig. 9-6). When the unit is dry, drill holes for the tension rods that run along the sides. Add the precolored rods (bits of wire), cutting them just a little short so nut, bolt, and washer casting (NBW) can be placed in the hole at the top. The little roller

at the base of the derrick is made from a few bits of plastic. Small pieces of wire rolled into a loop are used for eyelets. Some modelers use components from model ship rigging for pulley, eyelet, and rope detail. When all the detail is complete on derricks, mount them at the ends of the base, using a square to be sure they are perpendicular.

□ Just a few detail pieces are left. There are four tanks—actually two large air tanks (I used passenger car air tank castings) and two operating cylinders, simulated with short sections of dowels having small paper circles glued on the ends. A small rod with a circle of paper glued to the end acts as the piston in the cylinders (Fig. 9-7). These were mounted on the 6-×-8-inch-×-8-foot timbers. I did not groove them in place, although you might like to do so. The derricks need braces—plastic or paper strips painted a rusty red—and knee brackets. I used Walker Model Service castings, but again small pieces of plastic would work as well. The long boom with some bits of plastic at the base for a hinge were glued in place with super glue (Fig. 9-8). A small pulley at the top and a hook is all that is needed to finish the boom.

It's a good idea to spend some time at the hobby

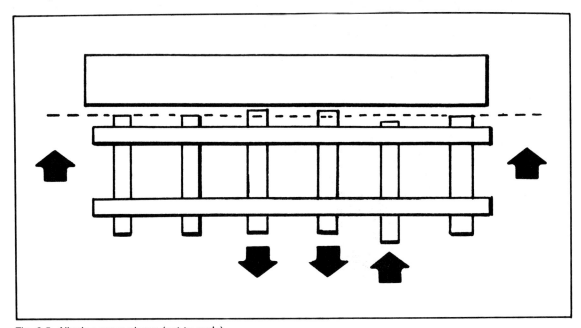

Fig. 9-5. Aligning cross pieces (not to scale).

Fig. 9-6. The base is assembled against a block or wood strip to keep all the cross pieces aligned. The derricks are assembled from strips and pieces of prestained wood.

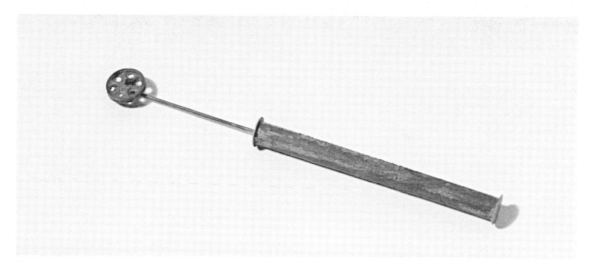

Fig. 9-7. The rails are lifted with air pressure and small air cylinders. Each cylinder was made from a piece of wooden dowel capped at the ends with a paper disc. The piston is a small piece of wire attached to a salvaged wheel casting, although another paper disc could have been used.

Fig. 9-8. All the metal-to-wood joints were bonded with an ACC adhesive called Super T, a thicker "super glue" that fills in wood and very rapidly bonds metal parts. The small teflon tube in the tip must be replaced frequently because it fills with Super T that hardens when not in use. Store in a sealed jar with silicon gel to keep moisture out.

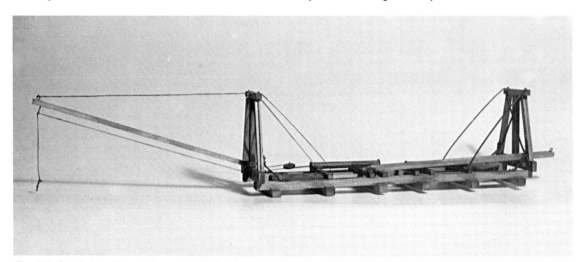

Fig. 9-9. Our finished loader has plastic strips for metal straps and thread for wires. I mounted only one of the booms to keep the length of the car down. The hook at the end was formed from a bit of wire.

Fig. 9-10. Now mounted in a service gondola, the rail loader is ready for heavy work on my Canadian Northern Railroad. If the railroad were a little more modern, I'd drop the loader off behind the roundhouse.

shop or browse through magazines and buy a few of the detail castings like pulleys, hooks, and NBWs to have on hand when you need them. Some times having a single part or not means the difference in finishing or not finishing a model.

□ The final step is stringing some thread for the wire rope, pulling it taut, and tacking it in place with little super glue. Unless you have a heavy weight at the end, model lines tend to look limp; so I like to leave them under a little tension and freeze that action with super glue. The choice is yours. Well, your car is finished. I'm parking mine on siding to wait for the next track repair project Figs. 9-9 and 9-10.

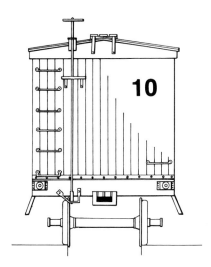

Building a Standard House Car

THEY CAME BY THE THOUSANDS, IN MANY shapes and forms, but all having a common ancestry—the house car. Call them boxcars, freight cars, lcl cars, or sometimes express and refrigerator cars, their design was fundamental—a wooden box, insulated if necessary, sometimes with fancy ends and roofs, but always the backbone of revenue service. The standard wooden boxcar is such a basic element, every railroad should have at least a few of them. In later years these wood cars became work cars and storage sheds, but I'll bet you could still find a few of them around today is you look hard enough.

The prototype for this project is a wooden ice car built by the Standard Steel Car Company of Pittsburgh, Pennsylvania for the Central Railroad of New Jersey. All the construction information was contained in a *Railway Age Gazette* article dated June 7, 1912. These old railroad journals can be excellent sources of information for building models. For example, there were several drawings of this car and information such as its width—8'6"; length

over end sills—38'4"; height—8'; capacity—140,000 lbs. of ice yet the car was loaded only to 80,000 lbs. because of a problem in shifting after the load began to melt.

Without mechanical refrigeration, the transporting of ice to remote areas was a real job for the railroads to protect produce, meat, and milk for shipment to the cities. For my model I took a few liberties, as usual, but I hope they are not too offensive to the purists among you. Study and measure the scale drawings in Figs. 5-4 and 5-5 to get a good idea of the car you will be building. Actually this basic box-type construction can be used for many different cars.

I began construction with a simple box made from two wooden end blocks and a flat top and bottom plate. All the materials are clear pine, cut on my father's table saw and made 1/16 inch shorter in all dimensions to account for the wood sheathing to be attached later. Once the pieces have been joined, sand all the surfaces smooth, especially where two pieces join. If you don't have access to a table saw, a simple box of 6-× -6 framing can be used (Figs. 10-1 and 10-2).

The sides are 1/32-inch-thick sheetwood with six scale-inch scribings. Long pieces of the scribed wood were cut and glued to the sides, allowing about 6 inches of the base to show and overlapping just slightly at the top. The exposed base will simulate the metal underframe. Be sure the pieces along the bottom line up straight and true. When the sides have completely dried, trim the excess off at the top and sand to meet the roof line.

The ends are also scribed sheetwood, cut slightly oversize but completely covering the ends. Again allow to dry, then trim back to the correct size. Do this slowly and carefully to just the right fit.

A 6-× -6 ridge pole is added on the top and is topped by additional 6 inch scribed sheetwood to make up the roof (Fig. 10-3). Leave a little more than 4 inches of overhang on all sides. Fascia of 6 × 1 1/2 is added along the sides, and 1 1/2 × about 12 inches at the ends is added. The end pieces must be cut, fitted, and recut to match the roof line and

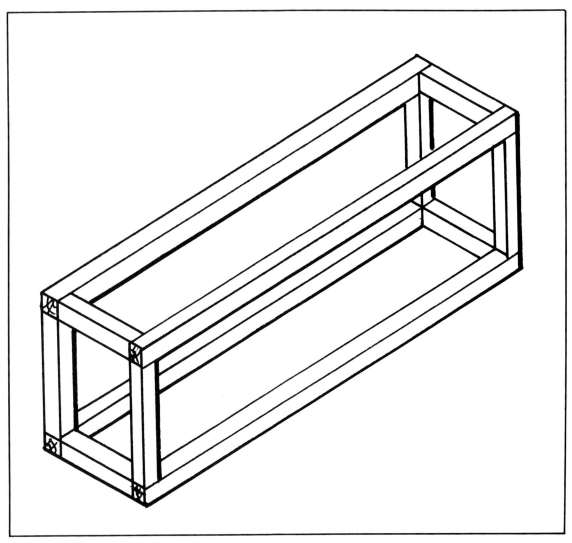

Fig. 10-1. Framing box.

Fig. 10-2. A simple wooden frame is used for the base of the model. All the edges are sanded very flat and smooth before the scribed sheathing is added.

Fig. 10-3. The box is covered with sheathing and sanded back to the top roof line. A 6- x -6 piece of stripwood is glued in place down the middle of the ceiling for a ridge pole, and 6-inch scribed sheathing is added as roofing.

also join with the side fascia. This step may take quite a bit of fitting and refitting, but a good joint will be worth it.

Finally the roof is cut back to a uniform overhang of about 1 1/2 inches on all sides. I placed a metal ruler that happens to be 1 1/2 scale inches thick tightly against the fascia and sanded the roof down until it just comes to the ruler (Fig. 10-4).

The roof walk was made in the same way as our kitbashing project in Chapter 8 by cutting small 2-×-2 supports, gluing them in place, and sanding them flat. Spray the entire model with your base color (in my case reefer white), lightly sand, spray a second coat of base color, then add the three 1 1/2-×-6 roof walk boards. To weather the car, use a stiff brush, place just a small amount of rather thick paint on the tip—a little from the bottle cap liner is fine—and sort of scrub on the second color. I used boxcar red. The more paint you apply, the less aged will the model appear. Finally the entire car is given a wash of black leather dye in rubbing

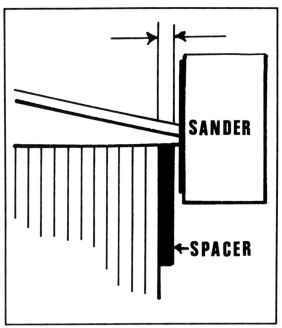

Fig. 10-4. Overhang space.

Fig. 10-5. After the basic box is finished with fascia and painted, lettering can be added. Some people may use decals for their favorite road, but I used commercial dry transfers, or *press-on-lettering*. Since no commercial lettering was available for the words *ice car*, art store alphabet sets were used. A knife is used to press the lettering into the grooves in the boards.

alcohol (just a little dye to a lot of alcohol) to act as a weathering stain and to tone down the colors.

When the car has dried, apply the lettering before you add any hardware. I used a set of commercial dry-transfer lettering for the general railroad name and lettering, and an art store set of white lettering for the words *ice car*. I hope you and all the Canadian Pacific fans will forgive me for mixing the Central of New Jersey bull's-eye with C.P. lettering, but it's my car, isn't it? Use a dull knife to push the lettering into the siding grooves (Fig. 10-5).

I still thought my car was a little too bright; so I further reduced the surface gloss by giving it a light sanding with fine-grade sandpaper. This step tore up a little of the lettering, but that really was okay as I wanted a really weathered car.

To drill the holes for all the grab irons which were bent from small bits of wire, I made a little plastic guide (Fig. 10-6) that could be held against the ends of the car so all the holes could be drilled at the same time. Each grab iron was bent in the jaws of a set of pliers and darkened with a chemical metal blackener. Several are available, but the most

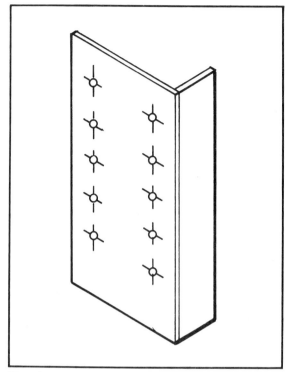

Fig. 10-6. Grab iron drilling guide.

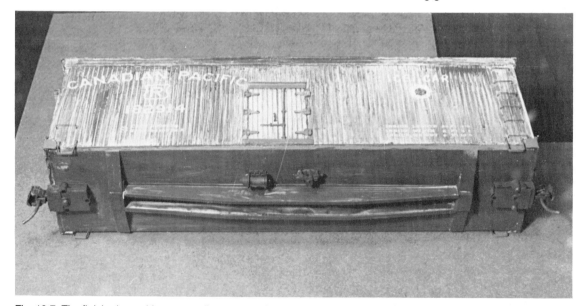

Fig. 10-7. The finished car with a very rudimentary under body detail in place receives two coats of black paint. The second coat will cover the remainder of the exposed raw plastic. The center sills are of the "fish belly" design, which means they rise from the bolsters, flatten along the middle of the car, then fall to the other bolster. I simulated them with thin plastic, with a small cap glued along each sill.

Fig. 10-8. The finished car will fit into any scene from 1910 to 1980. Two different styles of trucks suggest this is a work car using salvaged trucks.

common is Hobby Black. Care should be used with any of these chemicals, as they are generally quite poisonous. Just a touch of glue will hold the grab iron in place.

The side door hardware is a Grandt Line reefer door casting prepainted and epoxied in place. Short strips of thin plastic are placed above and below the doors. Since this is a refrigerator car, the doors are part of the walls and do not slide but swing open. The end sills are pieces of thin plastic glued in place and cut out for the coupler pocket (Fig. 10-7). Poling pockets are added near each end.

In case you don't know, the practice of *poling* a car into position involved placing a special wooden pole between the locomotive on one track and a car on an adjacent track. The pole had metal caps which would fit into a pocket on both the locomotive and the car. Although cars were not moved very far by this method, it did save a lot of excess moving by the locomotive, especially where the nearest turnout to move over to the next track, and therefore get directly behind the car, was some distance away. The practice proved to be very dangerous and was discontinued years ago. The pockets, however, remain on many cars even today.

About this time I was getting a little tired of this car so the underbody detail is minimal—it will never win a contest. I simply added two truck bolsters and a plastic "fishbelly" shaped underframe. Only a simple air cylinder and tank complete the undercar detail. If you want to improve the detail, consult any of the cyclopedias or other prototype sources for additional ideas.

The couplers were also added at this time by simply screwing them to the floor. I used Kadee automatic couplers, which seem to work very well for me. The underframe was brush-painted flat black, using two coats for complete coverage. The small car steps held in place with pins and a tall brake wheel (Grandt casting) complete the model. A little extra black weather stain and some tan-powdered tempera can be used to give the model an even further weathered look.

You'll note in the picture of the finished car (Fig. 10-8) that I mounted the car on two different styles of truck—one arch bar and one Bettendorf. Cars not in revenue service often get what's left, and salvaged, mixed, and unusual trucks are not uncommon. I hope you have enjoyed this project and will try scratchbuilding one on your own.

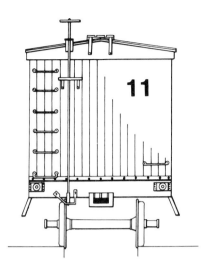

Working with Paper

MANY OF US MODELERS HAVE BEEN FORtunate to live in an era of fine-quality imported brass locomotives, beautiful castings, and an almost unlimited supply of structural shapes, parts, and components. Perhaps we should occasionally remember the "old days" when such a variety of materials was not available. Locomotive were frequently made from light sheet metal sometimes salvaged from cans. Tank cars were also made from cans of various types, and metal toothpaste tubes were unrolled, cleaned, and used to make a variety of metal parts for rolling stock. Cardstock was often used, too. Not the corrugated box material, but multiple-ply laminated sheets. Paper could be making a comeback in these days of high prices. Cardstock's limited popularity may be from lack of familiarity, rather than dislike for the material.

Cardstock has been used successfully to construct all types of models, including rolling stock and even interurbans (trolleys). Whether it is used alone or in combination with other materials, cardstock can be a very effective modeling medium. My personal choice is a particular brand called Strathmore board, a very high-quality paper made in single or multiple plies. Each ply is about 0.0005 inches thick and stocks ranging from one to five plies plus a1/16-inch-thick illustration board are available. Sheets vary in size up to 30 × 40 inches. When buying stock, be sure to obtain a hard-finished surface meant for ink rather than a textured or rough surface used with water colors or pastels. These rough-surface boards may have other creative modeling applications—use your imagination. Although more difficult to cut, the thicker stock may be used for car slides with a minimum of interior bracing.

WINDOW AREAS

For models with extensive window and glass areas, like long coaches or streamliners, a sheet of 1/16-or 1/32-inch-thick plexiglas may be used as the base for the entire wall. Cover the future glass areas with thin masking tape and then proceed to build up the model with layers of cardstock and wood glued directly to the plexiglas. When you are completely finished, including painting, the tape can be peeled back to reveal the clear window area. This lamination method provides a wall able to support the delicate scale window construction needed in many models where cardstock or wood alone would just not survive even the most careful handling.

SIMULATING WOOD AND METAL

Depending on your preference and project, cardstock can be finished to simulate wood or metal. Wood, as a porous substance, is very similar to cardstock. Cardstock can be scribed and stained to simulate wood as shown in the shed in Fig. 11-1.

To simulate metal takes a little more work. Since metal is nonporous, it is necessary to seal the cardstock, especially the edges. A good automotive body primer or wood sealer/primer can generally be used. You must spray it on three or more very light layers. Brush marks or unsightly runs and sags just do not resemble a prototype. A spray can with an adjustable nozzle is acceptable.

Many advanced modelers will eventually purchase an airbrush, which is a mini paint sprayer with adjustable pattern areas and spray rates. Pressure is supplied by a compressor or tank of compressed gas. Although it is not a tool for the beginner, an airbrush can eliminate all brush marks and provide very uniform coverage. Paints must be highly thinned for use with an airbrush, or problems in flow and surface coverage will develop. If you must use a brush, thin the paint thoroughly and apply several light coats, rather than one heavy one. Whatever method you use, it's a good idea to lightly

Fig. 11-1. This model, although primarily made of paper, has the look of weathered wood.

Fig. 11-2. This car features rivets, which are frequently used in older metal construction.

sand each coat after drying. Use a very fine grit—400 to 600 grit. The sanding will remove any small ridges and extensions of the sealer, leaving the valleys to be filled. After two or three coats and sandings, even a rough surface material will be smooth and sealed like metal.

The car in Fig. 11-2 features a number of rivets. Metal construction techniques, especially for older designs, require frequent use of rivets. They may be very easily simulated in thin cardstock by pushing in a series of small dimples or raised spots to form the rivet heads. I use a dressmaker's tracing wheel, which is a small disc-type tool with many small teeth on the edge (Fig. 11-3). I have also gone back to my junk box and found wheels and gears from old clocks and wrist watches and attached them to simple wooden handles to allow variation in spacing and size of the "rivets."

Place a semihard base like balsa or cardboard under the cardstock, then firmly roll the tracing wheel (or its equivalent) over the reverse side of the paper. Use a metal rule to guide the wheel. You may want to experiment on sample pieces of cardstock, using various bases and wheels to get the desired effect. Too soft or too hard a base will not allow the dimples to form properly.

Other modelers make rivets individually by drilling a series of holes in a thin brass plate then pressing the cardstock into the holes with a pencil point. With either method the rivets formed are susceptible to damage. If pressed, they will flatten and at least partially disappear. When you are painting the car, the rivets can be highlighted by rubbing them with a light or contrasting color. Commercial rivet punches are also available.

CARDSTOCK CONSTRUCTION TIPS

One ply of Strathmore is roughly 0.005 inches thick. Since an O-scale inch is about 0.020 inches, and an

Fig. 11-3. Dressmaker's tracing wheel and various gears used for pressing in ''rivets'' are shown.

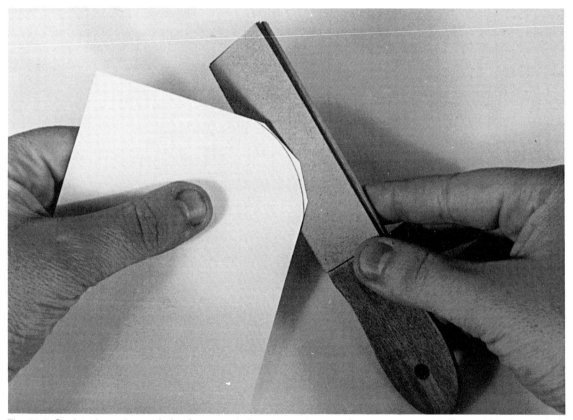

Fig. 11-4. Cardstock can be sanded to form rounded contours where a scissors or compass knife would be impractical.

HO-scale inch is about 0.010 inches, each ply equals approximately 1/4 inch in O scale and 1/2 inch in HO scale. Thus the scale thickness of any number of plies can easily and quickly be computed.

Cutting

Cutting cardstock is really quite an easy chore if you slice, rather than saw or chop, the stock. A very sharp single-edged razor blade is used, and because it is so thin, the blade will slice through very easily. A dull blade or heavier knife will push the material apart and tend to tear at the surface. Use a steel or metal straightedge held firmly in place while you make several light passes with the razor. Bearing down on the knife will only result in a sloppy cut, injured finger, or both. Thin stock up to about three plies can be cut with sharp scissors.

For outside curves, rough-cut the shape with several strokes of the razor, then finish with an emery board or sanding block (Fig. 11-4). For inside curved sections, such as the arched top of interurban coach windows, cardstock may be finished with a simple sanding block. Rough-cut the opening, leaving a little excess, then roll a piece of fine sandpaper around a dowel that is slightly smaller than the final opening. Sand to the finished size, then seal as needed.

Care should be taken to use a stiff board beneath the surface of the Strathmore. Too soft a base will allow the cardstock to bend down along with the knife and form a creased edge. The cutting board should have no grain (pressed wood is a suitable choice),so the razor does not wander off line following the wood grain.

Gluing

Many different types of glues will work with cardstock because it is porous. Water-based glues, like Elmer's, should be avoided, however, because warpage and ply separation will occur as the water is absorbed. A plastic cement like Testor's acetate cement (model airplane glue) has only hydrocarbon solvents and will dry without warping the cardstock. If you get a slower-setting cement, it will absorb into the paper surface before beginning to film over.

Rough the surface with sandpaper, then squeeze out a generous line of cement on the pieces to be glued. Don't try to spread the cement, because it will dry too fast. Cover the first piece with the laminate sheet and kind of smear this sandwich together, spreading the glue between the pieces. A little of the excess should ooze out the seam to show full coverage. Place a piece of wood or particleboard over the laminated sandwich to spread the force, and press with several large weights for at least 30 minutes to give the glue solvents time to diffuse through the paper and ensure a permanent bond.

Cardstock, like wood, has a grain; so it will flex more easily in one direction than the other. For greatest strength, the grains of the two laminated pieces should be at right angles to each other.

This lamination technique may also be used to make economic poster board by laminating a 1-or 2-ply Strathmore surface board to a less expensive cardboard back. Almost any thickness can be made by lamination.

Cardstock is a versatile and inexpensive material available in several formats. It is a good starting ground for developing your modeling skills. Let's go on now to some actual modeling projects that use cardstock as the basic modeling component.

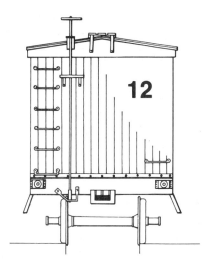

Maintenance of Way Equipment

IMAGINE YOU WERE OFFERED THE JOB OF maintaining the grounds of a major industry. We all need work, and cutting some grass or trimming a tree or two could not be that bad. Now imagine that the industry is the American railroad system with right-of-way through thousands of towns which get very unhappy if the weeds grow too high on railroad property. Your climate problems range from 300 annual inches of snow in Michigan's Upper Pennisula to subtropic swamps in Florida or the burning heat in Arizona's desert. Add to this the problem of keeping in true gauge the two steel rails that must stay 4 feet 8 1/2inches apart, or a roaring express with tons of freight may end up on the ties. The roadbed is constantly assaulted by water, wind, erosion, and rock slides. The rails must reach across streams, rivers, canyons, and chasms on bridges ranging from little wood platforms to steel giants. The job sounds a lot tougher now!

To meet these challenges the railroads have M O W (Maintenance of Way) and B & B (Bridge and Building) crews. They need very specialized equipment to clear off the snow, to set the rails in place, to shape the ballast, and to spray the weeds. One of the nice features of modeling M O W equipment is that they are very unusual, one-of-a-kind pieces of equipment that could be the jewels of the roundhouse scene. Also you need not model an entire blizzard to show that your railroad is in snow country. Just an old snow plow sitting on a weedy siding will easily convey the idea.

It's impossible for me to describe every piece of M O W equipment a railroad might use—many are homemade, many are modified commercial units. Instead I'd like to present a gallery of photos to show you the range of possible equipment you might kitbash or model from scratch. Enjoy!

Fig. 12-1. The *Big Hook* is the common name for the wrecking crane. When cars are on the ties or some big pieces of machinery have to be moved, these giants are brought out from their resting places hidden deep inside a roundhouse or yard building for a job no other piece of equipment can do. They are the 747s of the MOW roster.

Fig. 12-2. This big hook is a diesel-powered crane with a long boom that actually rests over a special car in front of the crane. Many times the extra (idler) car will carry trucks, track sections, and other items needed at a typical repair site.

Fig. 12-3. Although it was nearly dark, you can see this big hook—a steam-powered behemoth in the care of Mark Sacco at the Illinois Railway Museum. The crane has just lifted a small locomotive off a flat car and is preparing to put it down on the rails. Mark lowered it like a feather.

Fig. 12-4. This crane could be called the *little hook* since it's no bigger than a short flat car. Again steampowered, as many of the cranes still in use are, it was used on the Copper Range Railroad near Houghton, Michigan. Unfortunately this picture was taken of a scrap line.

Fig. 12-5. Also among the big brothers in the family of MOW equipment are the pile drivers. This C&NW unit is compactly folded up for movement. In operation the front tower arrangement unfolds and rises up above the car, and the entire body can rotate left or right. In operation the pile driver drops a huge metal weight on posts or pilings to drive them deep into the ground to reinforce the foundations for bridges, causeways, and similar construction projects.

Fig. 12-6. A much smaller type of pile driver was modeled by Charlie Dyxin in O scale. Here the unit is unfolded for operation, and the large drop weight can be seen about half way up the frame. This, too, is a steam-driven hoist, but probably for warmer climate judging by the open cab around the steam boiler. It might be used by a logging or small mining railroad in the South.

Fig. 12-7. Many different kinds of cars are used to bring ballast to repair or construction sites along the railroad. Currently I would expect to see old hoppers and gondolas that had finished serving their useful lives as revenue cars relegated to track service. This is my wooden model of a side dump gondola car with a peaked floor called an *A-frame*. Although this pitched floor reduced the capacity of the car, it allowed the ballast to easily pour out without using a clam shell type of crane. The car has a platform at only one end, probably for tools and small parts. The design is freelanced, but it follows the general features of a Southern Pacific workcar from about 1900.

Fig. 12-8. A close-up of the side shows that each of the small doors can be opened independently so the entire load was not dumped at one time but in quantities as needed.

118

Fig. 12-9. The end of a prototype side dump gondola shows the hinges on the side doors, and in this case the end has been removed. Also the brake wheel is missing; instead a ratchet type mechanism (Miner Brake Staff) is used in a very similar fashion to a socket set ratchet. The ratchet was much more compact and had less of a tendency to be damaged during work sessions than a high-positioned wheel.

Fig. 12-10. Once the ballast has been dumped, it must be spread. This machine is a cousin of the famous Jordan Spreaders, with folding wings and a plow in front just fitting over the rails. By adjusting the wings and plow, the ballast can be shaped to form a bed that will shed water and still hold the rails and ties.

Fig. 12-11. Once the ballast is shaped, a machine or men with forklike tools have to tamp it in place. This machine is a C&NW ballast tamper which automatically works the ballast in tightly around the ties.

Fig. 12-12. Sometimes ties have to be removed and replaced without taking up the rails. This handy little machine digs in under a faulty tie and cuts it in half so it can be pulled out in two pieces from either side.

Fig. 12-13. The cutting tooth on the end of a swing arm can be easily seen in this photograph. It would make an interesting model.

Fig. 12-14. Inspection is a never-ending job for the MOW crews, and many hours are spent in a little gas-powered scooter like this one.

Fig. 12-15. Believe it or not this is a railroad lawn mower. Along those places where only grass, weeds, and light brush follow the right of way, the C&NW will dispatch this super lawn mower. It can ride the rails on the small steel wheels just in front and behind the rubber tires, or completely lift off the rails and move about the adjacent right of way. The huge panlike objects in the front are the mowers, and they can be lowered on either side to do the cutting. These machines are used in towns and populated areas where spraying is not appropriate.

Fig. 12-16. For many of the railroads, snow is a mortal enemy, slowing the movement of trains, requiring extra crews, and in the extreme, actually shutting down the lines. This is a model scene I prepared using sifted baking soda as snow. The footprints are made with the eraser of a pencil (two per print). Few modelers recreate entire layouts with a winter setting, but it sure would be a challenge. By the way, the baking soda got into all the metal parts of this car, corroded them, and froze the trucks solid. How about flour or plaster?

Fig. 12-17. This wing plow, or Russel plow, was used by the Calumet and Heckla RR to fight the 300-inch annual snows of Upper Peninsula, Michigan. I just saw a virtually identical plow in Crystal Lake, Illinois in the bright yellow color of the C&NW; so it's quite possible that even the most modern railroad will have an old plow or two around. Often a plow is mounted on a gondola filled with sand or cement for counterweight.

Fig. 12-18. When the snow piles up so high or comes so often that the wing plows have pushed aside as much as they can, then the rotary plows are called into action. The rotaries are steam engines or diesels mounted on a frame and attached to a whirling blade in the front. This particular rotary was found on an abandoned spur in Michigan. It's lineage is unknown.

Fig. 12-19. The muscle end of the plow is where the whirling blades cut into the snow bank and pass the snow back to a fan blade just behind the front face. The fan throws the snow out through a chute, which can be adjusted to throw a huge plume of snow either left or right. In snow season, the rotaries are kept fired up 24 hours a day ready for action.

Fig. 12-20. Even after the rotaries pass, sometimes the snow is packed so hard against the walls of a cut that it forms an ice wall which the Russel plows cannot move. In that case a device similar to this "snow crab" is used. The wings or arms at the front are extended and the crab dragged backwards through the snow cut. The wings cut into the ice wall and pile the crushed ice in the center of the rails. A second pass by the rotary then throws the ice clear of the rails. For the next few snowfalls, the wing plows will again be able to push the snow off to the sides.

Fig. 12-21. A close-up of my model shows the grain and individual texture of the boards. The hinges were hand-rolled from soft metal.

Fig. 12-22. For snowfalls not quite so heavy, a simple plow like this one might be used. This homemade plow was used on the SOO Line.

Fig. 12-23. The front of the plow shows a borrowed headlight and a simple mechanism for raising the plow. This could be an interesting paper or plastic project.

Fig. 12-24. Finally one detail that is frequently overlooked is a flanger. In this case, it is a little trailing car used to clean out the list bit of snow between the rails and at the sides of the rails. Of course these blades must be lifted for turn outs, derails, and other obstructions in the tracks. Railroads will put marker signs along the tracks. Railroads will put marker signs along the tracks to warn the operator to lift the blades. I'd hate to have that job on this car out in the cold and wind waiting for the moment to lift the blades.

Fig. 12-25. Remember that just about anyplace a railroad needs to do track work will be far from the nearest supply site. Therefore tools, materials, supplies, and men must be transported and housed at the work area. This old boxcar, which we modeled in Chapter 8, has been downgraded to work train service on the CB&Q.

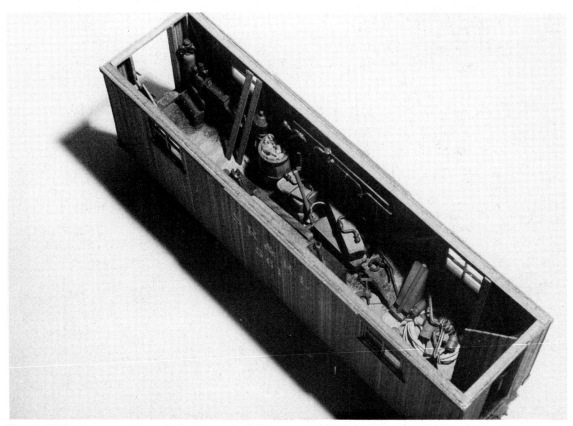

Fig. 12-26. Service cars give us plenty of opportunity for super detailing. Bob Brown added literally hundreds of detail parts for the "clutter" in this car (Courtesy Bob Brown collection of Wayne Wesolowski).

Fig. 12-27. This oil car won the Railroad Model Craftsman kitbashing award for January, 1983, for me and was a very interesting project. The body is a tender frame from an AHM Casey Jones locomotive kit, while the tank is a $.35 salvage table bargain at the local hobby shop (HO tank car). The box is just a few sheets of styrene. The original idea came from Paul Meier who had photographed a similar car on the Calumet and Heckla Railroad.

Fig. 12-28. This car built by Charles Dyxin probably shows how distinctive MOW equipment can be. An old-time tool car, it includes a boom, stabilizing jacks, several tool boxes, and counterweights, plus a winch. I wish I had built it. (Courtesy Charles Dyxin collection of Wayne Wesolowski).

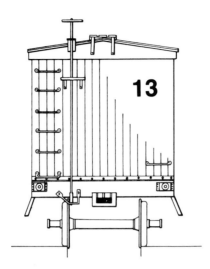

Building a Grease-Cleaning Car

LUBRICATION IS A WAY OF LIFE FOR THE railroads. Oils and greases are purchased by the drum and barrel and applied to rolling stock, motive power, stationary machinery, and even the rails themselves around tight curves. Sometimes, though, the grease that is almost everywhere has to be removed. You can only wipe so much off and then some kind of grease-cleaning agent, or degreaser, is necessary.

The degreaser is usually some form of solvent-based chemical that can be heated to dissolve the grease. Parts are dipped in the liquid until the oil coating dissolves and then the parts are hung up to drip dry. The solvent is used repeatedly until there is so much grease and oil in it that the bath can no longer be effective. At that point, the bath fluid may be sent off to a reclaiming firm that distills the degreaser from the sludge, or the entire bath may be discarded.

For the railroads with machinery in so many places, a portable parts degreaser would be very convenient. The prototype for the little car de-scribed here is the Santa Fe Railroad. I saw one photo of this type of car in a hobby magazine years ago and kind of "did my own thing" in designing the little car. It is nothing more than a small box with a little rivet detail in corners set on an old set of discarded trucks with no couplers or even springs. Construction time is about one evening, and since no dimensions are critical, even a first-time modeler should have no difficulty.

☐ Begin by laying out the entire car, including top and bottom, on a sheet of 2-ply Strathmore sheet or similar cardstock (Figs. 13-1 through 13-4). Cut this out with a very sharp knife, score the corners, and fold into a nice box with top and bottom.

☐ On a sheet of typing paper, lay out the corner brackets and impress the rivets with a clock wheel, dressmakers' tracing wheel, or commercial rivet press.

☐ Using a commercial solvent-based glue, such as contact cement, attach the corners to form the box and hinge the cover.

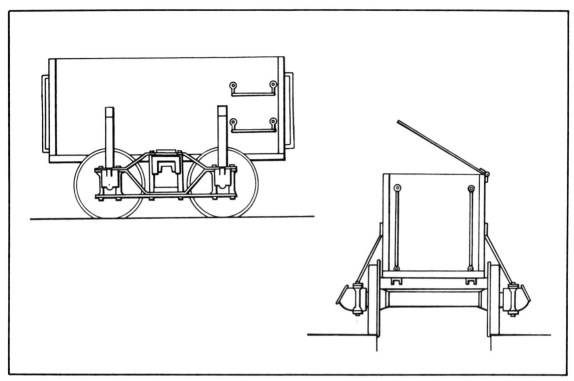

Fig. 13-1. Grease cleaning car (O scale).

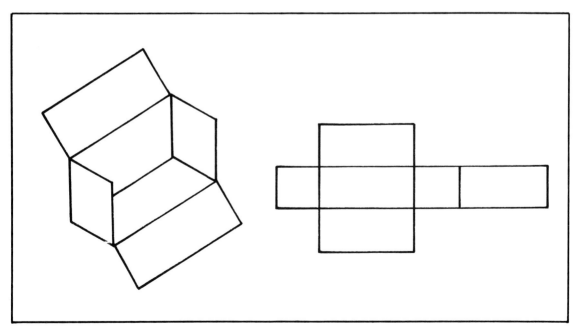

Fig. 13-2. Making the box (not to scale).

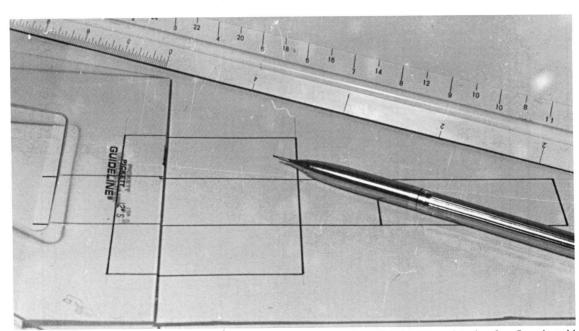

Fig. 13-3. Begin construction by laying out the car body on a sheet of 1-or 2-ply Strathmore cardstock; a 3- x -5 card would work as well. Use a T-square to make sure things are true.

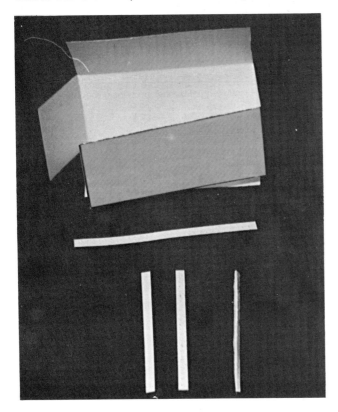

Fig. 13-4. Here the basic box is being folded. Small strips of typing or tracing paper with rows of rivets pressed in using a clock gear or tracing wheel are used for the corners. Prefold the corner pieces.

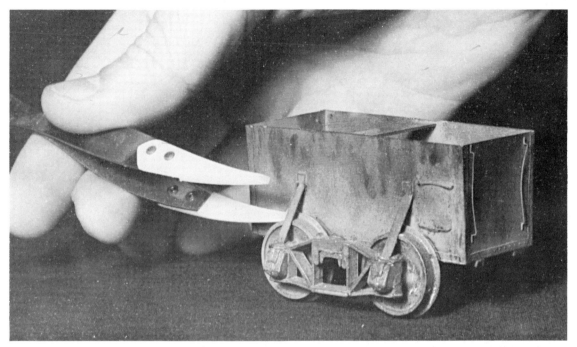

Fig. 13-5. Here the body has been placed on an old car truck with small pieces of plastic or brass used for the side supports. Notice there are no couplers. Men push the car to where it is needed.

Fig. 13-6. All the handrails are small pieces of wire bent in a set of needlenose pliers and pushed through small holes in the car. This car does not have a full top, but I plan to put a black plastic material in it to simulate the degreaser. The closed version is better for the beginning modeler since it would hide any openings or the ends of the grab irons. I would suspect the closed version would be likely in a modern scene, for environmental reasons.

Fig. 13-7. Our finished car has a really dirty look. The entire car was sprayed MOW (reefer) orange with lots of black weathering. Notice the springs from the truck are gone and only a piece of channel stock replaces the bolster.

Fig. 13-8. Don't worry if the grab irons are bent a little. This car was probably built from scraps and sees lots of hard knocks.

Fig. 13-9. The finished car adds a nice touch to a roundhouse or yard area scene.

☐ In your scrapbox find an old set of trucks—probably old archbar freight trucks that the railroad hasn't used in years (Fig. 13-5). If you're in a hurry, just use them as they are and glue the little box directly to the truck. To be a little more prototypical, remove the bolster and the springs and replace them with a single piece of brass or plastic channel stock simply glued in place of the bolster in the original truck.

☐ Add the hand rails for the top (Figs. 13-6 and 13-7).

☐ Paint the entire model with a bright color, like reefer orange or reefer yellow, but don't forget to add lots of black splashes or spills (Fig 13-8).

With just a little work, you should have a very respectable model to add as a little piece of detail to your roundhouse scene (Fig. 13-9).

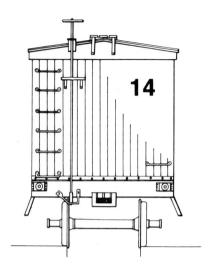

Building a Paper
Conrail Caboose

ERHAPS THE SINGLE MOST UNIVERSALLY accepted symbol of railroad nostalgia is the caboose. The UTU (United Transportation Union) of railroad workers presents a brass railroad lantern each year to the best model that captures the spirit of prototype railroading at the national NMRA meet. In what category? Cabooses, of course. The caboose, sometimes called a *crummy, waycar, hack,* and even worse by the men who work in them, is actually the headquarters of the train. It's the conductor, not the engineer, who is the head of the train. In the caboose he keeps track of orders and waybills and makes the decisions about what the switchmen will do. Some of these cars are quite comfortable; others rather miserable. There is always the problem of being jerked about at the end of a hundred-car train. Even with several coupler, when the slack comes out it can be quite a tug. I've ridden in the cabs of steam engines and back in the caboose. Both are significantly different experiences than sitting back with a paper heading into the city on a commuter express or even the

CTA in Chicago.

So that's why I've picked for our paper project building a little piece of this rail nostalgia. You know, there has been talk—even published reports—that with computers and the drive for more economy (smaller crews) the caboose may soon be out—replaced by a stick or flashing light and a computer—radio link. How sad!

Anyway, our model is of a Conrail metal way car that is a member of a large family of crummies all over the Northwestern United States. My guess is that several hundred of these cars were built from steel kits or similar designs for many eastern roads. They have been passed down and along to various lines through the years. For their complete history, you might want to consult articles in the July, August, and September 1982 *Railroad Model Craftsman* magazine and the March 1982 *Model Railroader*. These articles include many photographs of the variations.

Although we're building a basic caboose, you might consider some diversification, like using

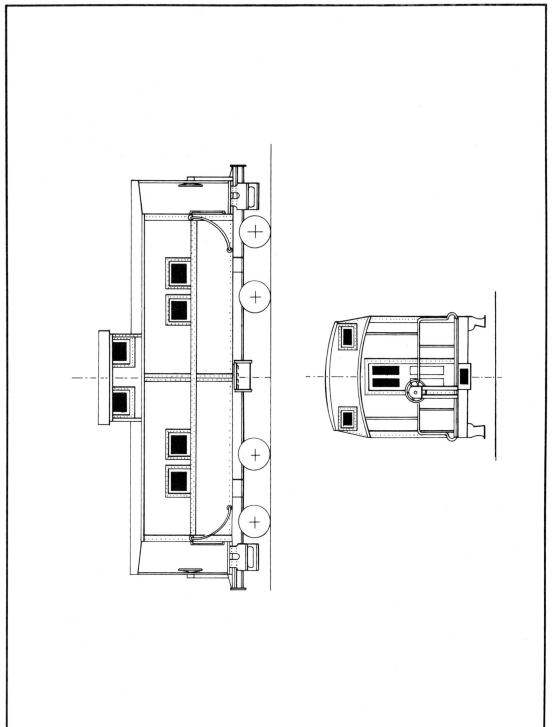

Fig. 14-1. Caboose (HO scale).

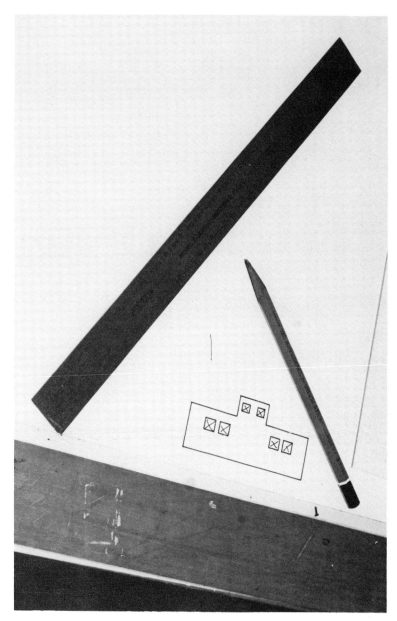

Fig. 14-2. Lay out the caboose on a single sheet of Strathmore.

round windows, adding a tool box underneath, adding coal stove pipes, covering some or all of the side windows with metal or window screen (for rock throwers), adding a roof walk and end ladders, or trying any number of paint scheme variations.

Let's get down to building.

☐ The body of the caboose is made from a single sheet of 3-ply Strathmore with overlays of 1 ply. Follow the plans in Fig. 14-1, and in one piece lay out the sides (Fig. 14-2). Don't do each wall separately. Draw a base line and measure all window openings and wall heights from it. Use a chisel-point pencil. The window opening should be to the trim only and not include the window itself. I cut out two interior walls that actually make up the

Fig. 14-3. All the caboose wall parts are measured against a common base line, scribed, and folded.

cupola faces at the top (Fig. 14-3).

    ☐ Place a piece of 1-ply stock under each window opening, then trace out the opening. Then with your pencil, mark off a second opening about 3 scale inches smaller (Fig. 14-4). When placed behind the wall make you window opening. With a very sharp knife, or, better yet, razor, cut out the openings. Use several light strokes and use a small file to

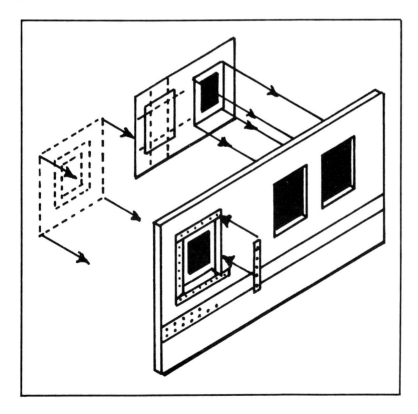

Fig. 14-4. Window opening (not to scale).

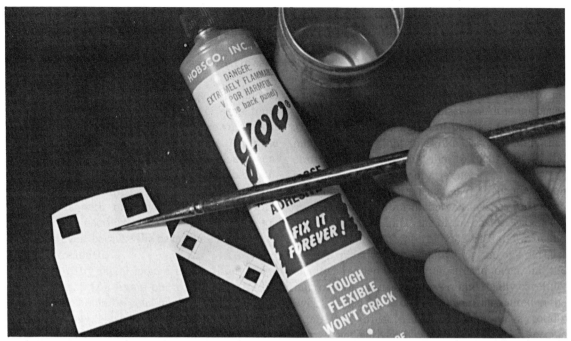

Fig. 14-5. The window inserts are attached with thinned GOO.

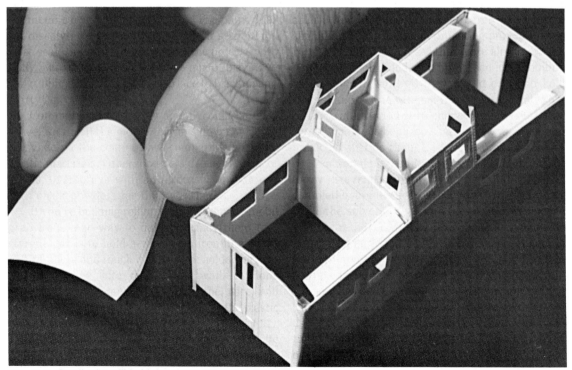

Fig. 14-6. Small tabs will hold the single-ply roof in place.

Fig. 14-7. I weighed my caboose on a garage-sale milk testing scale, but a postal scale would be just as good and much more common. Add weights as needed.

Fig. 14-8. The finished model will be an eye-pleaser at the end of any freight.

clean up any corners.

☐ To glue paper together, we need a thin, solvent-based adhesive, such as contact cement. Any white glue or water-based glue will cause wrinkling. I diluted Hobsco GOO about 50/50 with methyl ethyl ketone (MEK), or liquid plastic cement, using an old metal film can as a container (Fig. 14-5). Don't use a plastic one—it will dissolve in MEK—or anything that is not airtight. This liquid can be applied with a brush and leaves a fine film of GOO. Apply to both surfaces, blow dry, and press the two surfaces together. It is an instant set. Be sure the pieces are aligned because you won't get a second chance!

☐ The car has a great deal of rivet detail, which was simulated by representing in on a sheet of tracing paper with a clock gear. Use a steel rule as a guide and trim off the strip of rivets after they are pressed in. I messed up a number of rows, but that doesn't matter. It's easy to try again. Notice there are some double rows and some single. Each window is trimmed with a 3-inch-wide rivet sheet. Any excess glue can be "pulled up" by touching it with a toothpick and kind of twirling it.

☐ Using 1/8- × -1/8-inch pieces in the corners, fold the paper into a box and put some tabs along the walls to attach the roof. (Fig. 14-6)

☐ The roof is 1 ply with rivets along the edge.

☐ Sand the cupola top to get a tight fit with the roof.

☐ Spray paint the car with Conrail blue.

☐ The floor is 1/16-inch basswood sanded smooth and covered at the ends with a piece of gauze (buried in grimy black paint) to simulate the safety tread walks. The underbody only has a center sill, two bolsters, and a simple A-B brake cylinder and tank. Couplers are Kadee, and heavy spring caboose trucks were used. There is no roof walk or ladder on the modern version. All the handrails are fine wire painted yellow then pushed through small holes. The steps are tender steps, not the normal passenger steps.

Well, that's about it. Grab your lantern, signal the engineer, and let's roll out of town in your new caboose (Figs. 14-7 and 14-8).

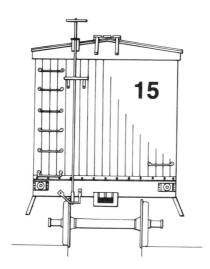

Working with Plastic

MOST OF US HAVE AT ONE TIME OR ANOTHer put together a plastic kit—maybe a train but also likely an automobile, boat, or novelty item. Although working with it was easy and rather straightforward, I never really thought much of styrene plastic as a scratchbuilding material. Perhaps I was too comfortable with using wood and paper as primary media for building that the idea of expanding into another type of material was disconcerting.

Several factors began to change that notion, however. Over the years I had seen excellent modeling done using styrene by such hobby experts as Al Armitage and Bob Brown that deep down inside I knew this material must have some value. Closer to home, Roger Witt, a model airplane afficionado turned model railroader, did amazing things in styrene, including simulating both wood and metal with seemingly equal ease. He even could draw tiny guy wires and electric lines by warming a piece of styrene rod in a candle flame and pulling the pieces, drawing out a thin filament that instantly

set into a very fine but rigid wire (Fig. 15-1).

I had built all-styrene models as early as 1970 (Fig. 15-2), but it really was a struggle, and they didn't seem to paint or finish as well as wood. Wood seemed to simulate wood best, and I was willing to leave it at that. Two manufacturers changed those ideas.

The first was Grandt Line, which produces an almost endless variety of super-detailed styrene castings for windows, doors, car parts, detail pieces, up to entire locomotives in O, HO, S, and even N scale. Since many of these are really not scale pieces—a small nut-bolt-washer (NBW) casting marked "O scale" actually can be used for a large NBW in HO—the possibilities are enormous. Since these castings were in plastic it seemed natural to use additional pieces of plastic to complete the model.

The real breakthrough, however, is the complete supply of dimension plastic materials available from Evergreen Scale Models. At your hobby shop is a virtual plastic lumberyard, with everything

Fig. 15-1. The modeling work of Roger Witt is clear in this excellent modified brewery kit.

from HO 1 × 2s to massive sheets 0.040 inches thick used for bases and bracing (Fig. 15-3). For a few dollars, you can have almost any size building material needed to make either a wood or metal model. By scratching with coarse sandpaper, an excellent wood grain can be achieved. By pressing with a blunt pin, rivet heads can be embossed in thin styrene for metal simulation. Commercial rivet punches are also available. Without the rivets, styrene easily simulates welded metal construction. Even bricks and roofing are possible without too much more trouble.

CHARACTERISTICS OF STYRENE

Let's look at some of the basic characteristics of styrene. Styrene is a petroleum-based polymer material that dissolves (softens) very readily in paint solvents. Although flexible, it will break very easily along a scored line. This feature makes styrene in-

credibly easy to cut and work. Simply score a light cut with a razor or very sharp knife, then snap along the cut, and the styrene breaks cleanly away. There is no need to saw or cut; just scribe and snap even for relatively thick pieces. This method reduces errors in locating dimensions, since you don't need to first mark a line in pencil then cut with a different tool. Circles and odd shapes are cut and snapped the same way, although very small circles (less than 1/4 inch) can easily be made with a ticket or paper hole punch.

A second characteristic of styrene is its ability to bond and dry almost immediately. A glue in the normal sense is not used. Rather two pieces of styrene are brought into very close contact, and a very small amount of solvent is applied with a brush. One of my early mistakes was to use a fancy syringe and apply too much solvent. This method leads to a mushy joint that does not set. The solvent actually softens and dissolves a little of each piece of plastic. They flow together slightly, and the solvent evaporates, leaving the plastic actually welded.

If the pieces are in good contact, very little solvent is necessary, and a strong joint is almost instantly made. I'm always amazed at the strength of a finished styrene model compared to a wood or paper one. If you apply too much solvent, a much longer waiting period must be allowed for the excess solvent to evaporate. There is also a good chance you will touch the softened plastic and leave an ugly fingerprint. Too little solvent is better than too much. If the joint doesn't take, just wipe with the solvent-moistened brush again.

Finally plastic is very easy to paint and finish. Being nonporous, it takes stains well without warping, and can be painted with most hobby paints with some caution. Paints like Flouquil's Polly S are primarily water-based and will not attack the plastic. Many other hobby paints are solvent-based and may soften or distort the plastic if they are applied too heavily. Several manufacturers offer a barrier or primer for plastics that will allow you to follow with almost any type of paint. The more layers of paint you apply, however, the greater the chance of hiding your detail. Therefore, I like to spray at least the base coat of any model. If they are sprayed in several light layers, even solvent-based paints can be applied without damage, provided the solvent is allowed to quickly evaporate. Actually the solvent action may dig in a little and give your coating a little better tooth for holding to the model.

Spraypainting requires some experience; so I would suggest experimenting on scrap pieces before you spray your best model. We'll talk about painting in more detail later.

Fig. 15-2. I built this model entirely from styrene sheet and strip in 1969 but gave up on styrene as a modeling material until a few years ago.

Styrene is by no means the perfect material for everyone. I frankly abandoned it for 10 years, but now I have enthusiastically returned to it. For metal simulation it is excellent; for very finely detailed construction it rivals the best wood construction. For ease and speed of construction it is excellent. Models that normally would have taken me months to build were completed in only a week or two because the parts were glued and dry as fast as I could assemble them. If you're a beginner, give styrene a try. It may be a very comfortable introductory material for you. You certainly can become an expert in almost no time. If you are a veteran, put the wood glue and soldering iron away for a week or so and try something new. I did and I was hooked for good.

STYRENE MATERIAL

As stated earlier, styrene is a polymeric material that's a basic off-white or gray, although it may be colored, depending on the manufacturer.

The styrene at your hobby shop comes in many different forms. The basic stock are sheets of either clear or white plastic in thicknesses ranging from 0.005 inches to about 0.040 inches; the most common sizes are 0.010 inches (1 inch HO 1/2 inch O scale) and 0.020 inches (2 inches HO, 1 inch O scale). Sheets of almost any thickness can be made by laminating together thinner sheets. You will need a good selection of the smaller sizes. I seldom use anything over 0.020 inches except for a base.

If you really fall in love with styrene, a more economical source for the simple sheet stock would be an industrial plastic supplier, usually listed under "Plastics" in the yellow pages of your telephone book. Several years ago I purchased four sheets of plastic a full 2 feet × 6 feet for only a few dollars. This stock will probably last my entire lifetime.

Generally the high-impact smooth surface styrene is most desirable. Many suppliers will have a $20 to $50 minimum order, which will buy an awful lot of plastic; so a co-op type arrangement with other modelers might be useful.

Back at the hobby shop, Evergreen Models supplies almost every size of cut styrene imaginable. For a dollar or two you can get a large package of HO 2 × 2s that are near-perfect in dimension and ready for use. The time saved in not having to cut all those pieces is well worth the cost. The table of scale-size conversions in Chapter 6 will help you use all the available sizes in different scales for your particular applications.

Also available are scribed sheets of styrene, which are wide pieces with V-grooves sliced along them to simulate many boards, as on the sides of a wall (the plastic equivalent of scribed sheetwood). Also available are clapboard siding and shiplap (novelty) siding (Fig. 15-4). The prescribed stock saves a great amount of time in cutting all those boards.

An interesting product is car siding, which is scribed vertically along a long strip of plastic. The pieces are generally long enough so an entire car side can be made from a single piece without having to butt pieces together—a nice time-saving feature.

Evergreen continues to introduce new styrene products, such as roofing, sidewalk pieces, and special scribed pieces. Talk with your hobby dealer about them.

Another supplier of plastic material is Plastruct, Inc., which supplies material to the professional modeling fraternity, especially piping, and chemical and nuclear plant design models. They have numerous structural shapes such as I-beams, H-columns, pipes, rods, elbows, and valves. The plastic material is general ABS (acryl butyl styrene), which is tougher than styrene and does not bond as quickly.

Many of their parts are very small, like 1/32 channel stock, but have a rather thick cross section. I believe this is because the parts are extruded or drawn through a die to the shape of the final part. With this process, some rounding of the corners and thickening of the webs will occur. The thick webs will not take rivet detail well; so for very precise structural shapes, I make them up from strips of styrene (Figs. 15-5 and 15-6). For larger projects or those where the detail is not critical, I would not hesitate to use Plastruct.

Another good Plastruct product is the wide

TWO SHEETS   1/4 INCH SCALE

peel and stick....

PAVING BRICK

IHR8904-1

"looks and feels like the real thing!"

ILLINOIS HOBBY CRAFT INC.

METAL SIDING

THICKNESS .040 IN.
SPACING .060 IN.
4527   E

evergreen scale models

StripStyrene
12 Pieces
HO Scale 1x8

8108

8106

Fig. 15-3. Plastic-based materials are available in many types, styles, and forms.

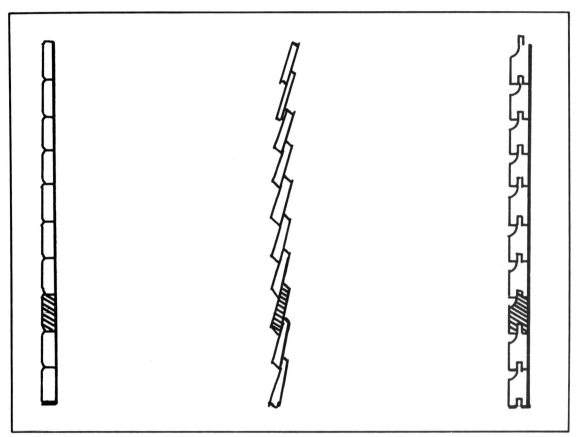

Fig. 15-4. Scribed, clapboard, and shiplap siding.

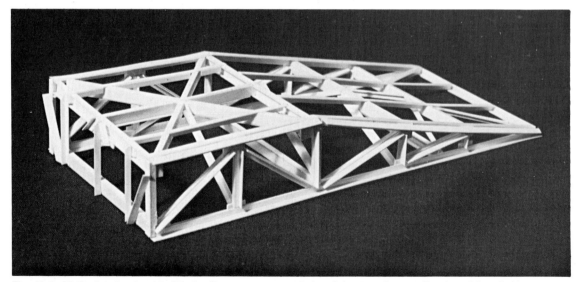

Fig. 15-5. All the framing for this little loading ramp was made by gluing together small strips of 1- x -3 styrene.

Fig. 15-6. The finished model loading ramp is all styrene construction and simulates metal very well.

selection of tank ends—dished, elliptical, and hemispherical, along with the correct size plastic tubing to fit the ends (Figs. 15-7 and 15-8); so there is no more need to hunt around for paper towel tubes trying to make a tank or a gasoline storage tank. Your hobby shop may not stock the tank ends, but you can order them.

COMPONENTS AND CASTINGS

The widest variety of plastic components are the many plastic castings available from Grandt Line, Gould, Walthers, and others. These are all compatible with the basic styrene materials. I hesitate to even attempt to describe the variety of parts available. Windows, doors, hardware, NBWs, car parts, roof vents, water tank parts, people, ornamental iron work, and railings are just a few of the items that come to mind. Just browse through the catalogs of the major manufacturers and start building a collection. For scratchbuilding cars, you will want to collect a lot of NBWs of different shapes and sizes, as well as the basic car parts, such

as coupler pockets, side pockets, and brake wheels. I have two full shoe boxes of parts. Compared to brass castings, these parts are very inexpensive, usually less than $1.00.

The final source is one that every scratch-builder eventually considers his or her best—the good old scrap box. My own scrap box is filled with pieces of unfinished projects, kits my boys tossed, small plastic boxes, even the sprues from toy castings which can be put to use.

Almost nothing is wasted when you are working in plastic. Commercial plastic castings are probably the easiest to modify for special applications. For example, the special door in Fig. 15-9 can be made by taking a standard five-panel door and trimming along the side and the arched window at the top. The entire process took only a few minutes, yet the result is excellent.

I keep a scrap box of old castings that might have been painted or prepared for a project, then not used. When a project calls for a window but I'm not too particular, I go first to the scrap castings box before opening a new package of castings. This

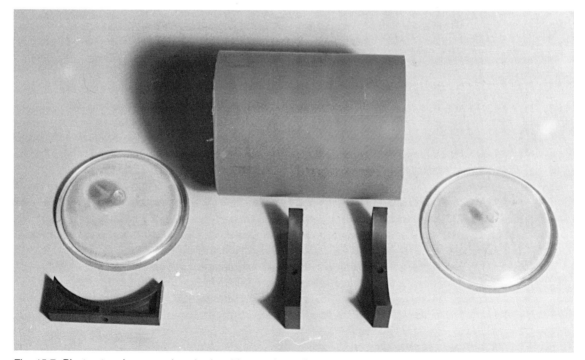

Fig. 15-7. Plastruct makes very nice plastic tubing, ends, and supports.

150

Fig. 15-8. Using the tube and ends, this fine old-time tank car model was made to fit on a styrene and wood base. The prototype car hauled concentrated sugar solutions for an Illinois firm in 1908.

Fig. 15-9. Neither of these parts are available commercially, but were made by gluing together two or more plastic castings and adding bits of styrene where necessary.

step eliminates the tedium of trying to refile any casting not used. My only filing system is to put a rubber band around similar casting packages and keep a general organization: NBWs in one place, doors in another.

Clear styrene makes an excellent window glazing material that can be cut easily and attached with just a touch of your styrene solvent (MEK) brush. Don't use too much, or it will frost the window. Watch out for fingerprints; use thin cloth gloves.

It's also easy to make broken and damaged windows by scribing with a sharp X-acto knife. Bullet holes can be made with a small drill, afterwards scoring the fine cracks away from the hole. I borrowed this idea from Shep Paine's article on building model jeeps for military dioramas in *Fine Scale Modeler*, a monthly magazine for miniaturists. It never hurts to see what the airplane, dollhouse, and miniature people are doing.

Plastic also comes in large sheets embossed to represent bricks, stone, flagstone, rock, and other surfaces. Both Holgate/Reynolds and Illinois Hobby

Craft make brick materials in several scales.

Perhaps one of the more interesting applications of plastic is the modular car sections sold by the Indianapolis Car Company (ICC) (Fig. 15-10). The manufacturer produces styrene injection-molded car sides and ends, windows, doors, arched baggage doors, and many others. Side rails and letter boards are cast into each module; so you need only mix and match the number of windows, doors, and blank sections you need to make the finished model. ICC even sells a clear styrene car roof with the ends already perfectly curved and slotted to fit their end pieces—a quick and easy way to almost scratchbuild the trolley or passenger car of your choice.

BONDING

There are several commercial products used to bond styrene, but I prefer methyl ethyl ketone, which can be purchased in pint quantities at your hardware store. The commercial agents tend to be

152

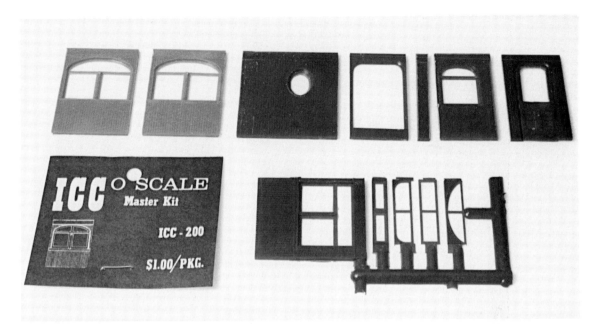

Fig. 15-10. Entire passenger cars or trolleys can be assembled from these plastic modules available from the Indianapolis Car Company.

mixtures of materials that give a longer setting time. I actually like the very rapid setting action, and you can't beat the price. The solvent does have a "heady" kind of odor, and I would use it in a well-ventilated area to avoid any health problems. Should you develop a rash or feel dizzy or ill, immediately discontinue use of the material. Store your MEK in a wide-mouthed, low-profile bottom that seals tightly and is not likely to tip over.

Whenever applying solvent, it is best to try and hold the pieces in such a way as to prevent the solvent from escaping and spreading to other areas, such as the bench top (Figs. 15-11 and 15-12). With very small pieces, solvent may overflow, or the

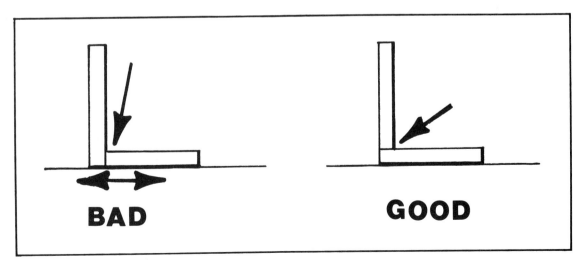

Fig. 15-11. Solvent application.

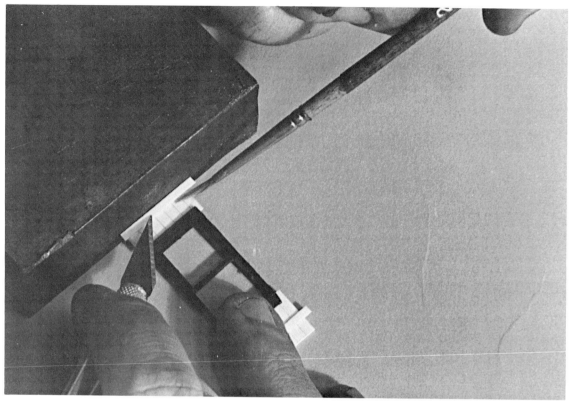

Fig. 15-12. This is the technique I use for gluing styrene. The parts are held tightly against a metal weight, while the solvent is sparingly applied with a brush.

pieces may stick to the bench. If they do, it is no disaster—just slide them along a little to break the solvent bond and then allow to dry. Avoid handling as much as possible, but just that slight movement will keep the part from fusing to the bench.

Should you choose to use a "plastic cement" that is heavy-bodied, be very careful as many of these are mixtures of MEK and a large amount of dissolved plastic to act as a "builder." The problem with these adhesives is that they continue to keep working and dissolving the plastic long after the bond has set. I've tried to glue sheet styrene to other surfaces with a few blobs of plastic cement here and there only to find the model had developed pock marks and pits after setting overnight. The lumps of glue had dissolved through the sheet styrene. For gluing styrene to other materials, such as wood or metal, I would use an adhesive like Hot Stuff or Super T.

Basic tools for styrene include the same set that we suggest in Chapter 3, but I would add a hard cutting surface like glass or Masonite to keep the edge of small strips of plastic from bending and fraying under your hobby knife. You will also need a steel ruler with some sandpaper glued to the back. Plastic has a very slippery surface, and it's difficult to hold a ruler steady. You'll also need a fine brush to apply the solvent. Be careful about using cheap, plastic-handled brushes, as they may dissolve in the MEK you are applying.

FINISHING

Finishing makes the difference whether styrene looks like wood or metal. For wood I scrub the surface with a light sandpaper, with the edge of a zona saw or with a wire brush. Try to simulate a grain running along the length of the wood (Fig. 15-13).

154

Fig. 15-13. Styrene can easily be used to simulate wood, as in my model of this elevated shanty.

Knotholes can be made with a small drill, and boards broken at the edges with a sharp knife. For a smooth finish, only a brushing or spraying with the base color is necessary. There is no need to sand between coats.

For a more aged look, I like to coat the model first with a base coloring, like a gray or beige tone, then give a second coat of a rustic brown or boxcar red, and finish with the final coating. After the paint has set, take a little MEK on a brush and gently scrub the surface, exposing the layers beneath. This step takes a little practice, but gives a terrific aged effect with old layers of paint showing through. Don't scrub too hard or use too much solvent, however, because the base white styrene can easily be reached.

For a rusty metal look, I use a different approach (Fig. 5-14). Again put a base coat on, but this time it should be your final color. Allow it to dry thoroughly. Next put out a small container of rubbing alcohol (isopropyl alcohol). Take a brush and just dip it into some Polly S "rust" and then into the alcohol. Apply this mixture in blotches to the metal car in a random fashion. The paint does not dissolve well in the alcohol, and it settles in a loose scale, much like rust. Repeat the process with Polly S boxcar red. Finally flow a mix of black dye and rubbing alcohol over the surface to blacken and "dirty" it even more.

Commercial weathering agents could be used as well to finish the model. Always do it sparingly and check if the coatings are compatible with the plastic materials. Other modelers use light coats of paints, oversprays with an airbrush, or dustings with chalk powders for final weathering.

If you're building rolling stock with many metal grab irons, one way to quickly attach them to a styrene car is to hold a wire grab iron in a small pair of pliers and touch it with a hot soldering iron while pressing into the plastic wall. If done carefully, the plastic will soften, the wire will penetrate, and when the iron is removed, the plastic will solidify around the metal.

The hot soldering iron can be used to make very effective dents and wrinkles in the plastic.

Hold the iron close until the plastic softens, but don't touch and burn it (Fig. 15-15).

MOLDING PLASTICS

The final area that modelers have begun to investigate is the molding of plastics. Although there are many different types of plastics available for modelers from companies like Castolite and other craft suppliers, I would like to focus just on the molding, or forming, of styrene.

Sometimes there is a need to bend or roll styrene sheets to form curved surfaces for tanks, fenders, and the like. One of the easiest ways is to use simple boiling water. I once tried to warm and bend a plastic cast window for an old derelict shanty. I tried heating it in the oven, in the microwave, with a hair dryer, and finally carefully over an open flame on the stove. All resulted in the same two effects—either nothing or a totally warped and shrivelled casting. Plastic has a specific softening point that is hard to capture in the home shop. I finally submerged it in boiling water and after a few minutes could just barely push it to a slight curve. Further experimenting proved I could bend and hold thin pieces that were already rolled over a form, clamped, and immersed in the boiling water. When removed they would cool and hold their shape. Trying to just heat a piece, pull it out of the water and curl to shape proved fruitless.

If styrene is bent too sharply, it will crack and break off just as though it was scored.

For small pieces like thin strips you may want to try "solvent shaping." The piece of styrene is completely immersed in MEK for 10 to 30 seconds while the solvent seeps into the plastic. When the piece is removed, it's as flexible as a wet noodle and can be curled into almost any shape. If held in position and allowed to dry, the piece will retain the final position. This method can be used for rolling small rings of styrene or for folding and rolling the corners and braces of early metal cars which used pressed metal structural parts that were eventually riveted together. One caution: gently blow on the piece when it is removed from the solvent

Fig. 15-14. This mineral concentrate car was built entirely of styrene again using small strips and pieces to make the angled parts. All the grab irons were positioned by heating pieces of wire with a soldering iron and gently pushing them in place.

Fig. 15-15. A soldering iron was used to create the dents and creases near the top edge of this car.

Fig. 15-16. Al Westerfield made the masters from styrene for this beautiful auto car, which was then cast from a liquid plastic resin for commercial sales. Even the tiniest rivets are reproduced in HO scale (Courtesy Al Westerfield from the collection of Wayne Wesolowski).

to quickly dry the surface so any touching or forming will not severely score the surface. This method must be classified as experimental, but it can make some beautiful parts.

Several years ago Mattel manufactured a toy called a Vacuform which heated small squares of styrene and pulled them over a pattern using a small hand vacuum pump. If you find one of these units at a garage sale or flea market, you could start into custom vacuum forming with your own patterns.

Finally there is the actual molding of liquid styrene in rubber molds. Although it is a little beyond the level of this book, I'd like to make you aware of the process and its potential.

For years modelers have been making castings in materials like plaster, polyester resins, and epoxies (Fig. 15-16). The process involves making an exact master of your particular part then pouring a liquid-type rubber material around the master. When the rubber (I use Castomold SR/P from Castolite Company) has hardened, the master pattern is removed from it, leaving behind a cavity that is the exact size of the original. If the cavity is filled with plaster, liquid resin, or epoxy, a copy of the original is produced. The drawbacks are that plas-

ter breaks easily; resins have terrible odor problems and shrink considerably, and epoxies tend to adhere to the molds and tear them.

Recently modelers have been filling the molds with styrene chips (Castochips, Bakin' Beads and others), placing the entire unit into the kitchen oven, and heating until the beads melt and fill the mold. The main drawback to this method is styrene castings are normally made under pressure with the softened plastic being squeezed into a die. In the kitchen oven method, the only pressure is that of the liquid plastic, which may not be enough to reach the small corners of the mold. The primary advantage, and it's very important, is that your finished castings are normal styrene and can be bonded, worked, and handled like any piece of plastic, needing no special glues, agents, or special handling. I'm sure modelers will carry the study of this method far; perhaps you might like to try.

With so many options, you can see why styrene is becoming the modeling material for many hobbyists. If you'd like to test the waters, we have two projects for you—a simple one and one a little more complex. Study the techniques in these projects, and you'll be well on your way to scratchbuilding or kitbashing in styrene.

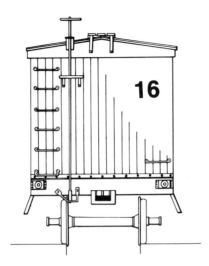

Passenger Car

W HILE I WAS ATTENDING SCHOOL IN THE East 15 years ago, I had the marvelous experience of traveling between Chicago and Boston on the train. It actually was little more than an overnight trip, leaving Chicago's Dearborn Street station in the late afternoon and arriving in Boston late the next morning. For me, though, it was an exciting adventure that is becoming increasingly harder to find.

The real history of passenger cars begins about 1830 and actually ends in the 1940s. Although cars are still being built for suburban commuter service today, the real development stage of passenger cars ended with World War II. This reflects the fact that from about 1860 until about 1930 the railroad passenger car was, by far, the major means of long-distance travel for all Americans. The peak was reached sometime slightly before World War I, and ridership has fallen steadily since then, making the need for new cars moot. Car development is a fascinating study of the way an industry looked at the problem of moving people. Competition be-

tween parallel lines brought on developments such as luxurious parlor and dome cars. An excellent book on the subject is *A History of the American Passenger Car* by John H. White Jr.

From a modeler's viewpoint, we are more interested in the exteriors of cars, but many times these visible areas actually are shaped by the design elements of the interior. We'll offer specific projects later on, but let's look for a moment at the development of the passenger car.

EARLY PASSENGER CARS

In the 1830s, the passenger car was nothing more than a stagecoach equipped with railroad wheels. With only four wheels and a minimum suspension system, the ride was terribly uncomfortable. In addition, the cars were basically wide open, and steam, smoke, and the elements assaulted the passengers.

Joseph Smith and the B&O Railroad are credited with introducing the first eight-wheel car—the Columbus. It was actually a box about 30 feet long and 8 1/2 feet wide, with only a 6-foot head clearance. The big development was to use two four-wheel trucks at each end of the car and thus tremendously improve the ride, increase capacity, and allow the car to traverse rather rough or curved trackage. It weighed only about 8 tons and cost less than $2000. Perhaps not in the best interests of the rider, the small boxlike cars were dictated by the general conditions of the purchasers.

In the 1850s, trips extending up to 500 miles became common, and the passengers could simply not survive these trips in the smaller cars. Car sizes grew to about 40 feet, and some creature comforts like heating stoves were added for the passengers. To support the larger cars, center sills or main support beams were added up the middle of the car floor. Also the sides of the cars were made with side-panel trusses, an idea drawn from bridge construction. These light, but very strong, trusses allowed increasingly longer spans to be constructed without adding excessive weight. Cars now approached 10 to 12 tons.

VENTILATION

One of the problems that plagued passengers until the time of air conditioning was "bad air." To assist in ventilation, a small extension of the roof was made in the 1860s. This center section, called a *clerestory* rose about 18 inches above the rest of the roof and with ventilators in the sides provided both air exchange and additional lighting. The first cars had square or monitor ends that must have offered tremendous wind resistance. Later designs pointed the clerestory much like the prow of a ship. Finally the designers simply curved the roofs down to meet the main roof.

In earlier designs the clerestory met the main roof several feet short of the end of the car. These were generally known as *duck bill roofs*, while the more modern cars had the clerestory continue directly to the end of the car before dropping down. These roofs are called *crescent*, or bullnose, roof ends, (Fig. 16-1) and became the standard in the 1870s. The clerestory did improve lighting and ven-

tilation, but the change in roof line also significantly weakened the roof structure because designers did not want to break the open spaces inside the car by adding additional roof trusses.

There were no major structural changes between 1860 and 1875, but if you enjoy building ornate and detailed cars, this is your era. A multitude of architectural features were added to cars, including delicate finials, ornate oval side frames, car names, arched windows, stained glass, and interiors of regal elegance. These cars are seldom modeled, but when someone does the research and the work, the response from modelers and judges is overwhelming.

As cars continued to grow longer, the demand for high-quality lumber increased to the point where forests in the northeastern United States were depleted, and trees were no longer tall enough to be used for a single framing piece. Extensive splicing became necessary for cars over 60 feet, and trussrods with queen posts became common. The *queen posts* were metal castings that supported along truss rods which ran the length of the cars and through the end sills. By tightening these rods both at the ends and with mid-body turnbuckles, tension could be applied to the car body, helping it to support the extra weight of the car and prevent sagging.

METAL CARS

By 1900, the 80-foot wooden car was about the limit of the woodworking craft. Railroads had been using metal in freight cars since the late 1880s; so it was natural to transfer this material to passenger cars. The change was neither swift nor complete. Craftsmen and companies who had worked with wood for years were reluctant to make the philosophical changes to metal. When the Pennsylvania RR made a commitment to steel cars in 1907, the change was inevitable. Surprisingly by 1920, 60 percent of the cars in service were still wooden. What had happened is that the wood cars were simply downgraded to local service and then to maintenance service, but they were not scrapped rapidly. This is a boon for modelers, since

Fig. 16-1. The Bull End or Crescent End complete the roof line of the clerestory on this car. On more ornate old-time cars, the upper section would have fine, leaded-glass windows.

it means you have an excuse for using a wood car even on a very modern railroad. You can pick almost any kind of car and justify its use on your pike.

At first the cars were *composites*, that is, a mix of wood and steel. Eventually, however, all-steel frames and bodies were constructed. Although stronger than wood ones, the early metal cars were subject to a very serious hazard. Because of the strong frames and relatively weak bodies, in a collision one car might lift up and drive right through the body of a second car. This condition of one car sliding inside the body of a second was called *telescoping*. In 1913, Barney and Smith introduced a collapsible car end that would absorb some of the impact of a collision. In an entire train the force of collision would be spread down the train in these collapsing ends, rather than focus it at the point of impact. Heavy steel beams were added to the ends, keeping cars from rising up and crashing through the top of the adjacent car, which was called *high-level telescoping*.

These all-steel cars, called *heavy weights*, operating on two sets of 6-wheel trucks needed a great deal of insulation because the metal was a good conductor of both cold and sound (Fig. 16-2). The floors were frequently made from a reinforced layer of asbestos and cement. Not all the cars had the traditional clerestory, such as suburban coaches made by the Standard Steel Car Company for the Harriman Lines including the Rock Island, Union Pacific, Southern Pacific, and Illinois Central.

THE STREAMLINERS

The last phase of passenger-car construction was the era of the streamliners (Fig. 16-3). It was not so much a revolution in design as in materials and construction techniques. Generally, streamlining meant rounded corners and airflow lines on usually lighter cars. The changes in design were forced to some extent by competition between railroads for the remaining passengers who instead on moder-

Fig. 16-2. A heavy-weight passenger car required large 6-wheel trucks but gave a very smooth ride.

Fig. 16-3. The queen of the passenger streamline cars was the solarium observation lounge. This Milwaukee Road Hiawatha was retired to the scrap line but still has the grace of a streamliner.

Fig. 16-4. A common site around large cities with commuter railroads are the double-deck gallery cars for short-haul passenger service.

nization and increased comfort. Almost universal air-conditioning and the vista-dome cars are examples of market-driven changes. The changes were slow in coming, similar to the replacement of wooden cars. Even in 1948, old heavy weights with rivet construction and six-wheel trucks were delivered to the Alton Railroad.

Several new materials were introduced, including aluminum, "Cor-Ten" steel, and stainless steel. Aluminum never proved successful because it was frequently combined with other materials, which eventually caused corrosion problems deep inside the car bodies.

Budd was the first to build entire cars from stainless steel—a very strong, but light and ductile, alloy. The invention of the Shotwelding process made the use of stainless possible. Cars constructed from this material were very expensive, but lasted almost indefinitely. The Denver Zephyr was overhauled in 1949 after 4.5 million miles of service with no signs of deterioration in the body or framing. The Burlington Zephyr built in 1934 is still

in excellent condition and is on display at the Museum of Science and Industry in Chicago.

The light weights never really replaced the heavy weight cars because of the general decline in rail passenger business. Some roads took to repainting their heavy weights with *shadow lining*, a technique to make the smooth-sided cars appear to have the streamlining. Rapid transit and suburban light weights continued to be constructed into the 1960s. Interest in mass transit spurred by the oil crisis may again increase car construction. In 1950, the Burlington received thirty 85-foot double-decked "gallery" cars for commuter service in the Chicago area (Fig. 16-4).

SUMMARY

Over all, the construction of passenger cars never followed typical designs. From 1945 to 1950, more than 3700 cars were built to over 420 different designs. This kind of diversity is ideal for the modeler, since you may be able to find a style and design of passenger car that suits your needs. In general, construction was based on a long tradition of excellent craftsmen—cabinetmakers, wheelwrights, foundry workers, drapers, painters, and many others. Designers were very conservative and tended to react to new materials and ideas rather than generate them.

In this short discussion, we've left out a wide range of special cars that served along with the passenger coach. There were diners, baggage cars, generator cars, sleepers, observation cars, and the famous Pullman cars—parlor car and smokers serving special clientele. Perhaps the most interesting of all—the private car—would make an excellent area for you to investigate on your own. How about a private car for the officers of your railroad? You can make it ornate or strikingly utilitarian. The choice is yours. The passenger car offers you many modeling options.

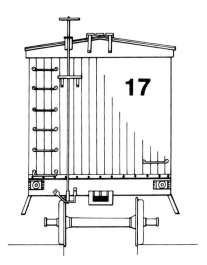

Building

Pulpwood Gondola Braces

AS A RAILROAD'S REQUIREMENTS CHANGE, sometimes only a simple adaptation or modification of rolling stock can easily fill that need. One example is the Chicago and Northwestern's need for cars to carry pulpwood logs from the forest to the paper mills. Ideally the logs would be transported in specially designed bulkhead flat cars or rack cars that allow the logs to be stacked quite high.

One problem that arises is that this kind of traffic is seasonal and rather sporadic at best. Depending on the national economy and other factors, they may move a lot of logs or not many at all. Clearly the investment of millions of dollars in a fleet of specially designed log cars is not justifiable. Rather some way to modify existing equipment is needed. I stumbled across the cars in Figs. 17-1 and 17-2 alongside the depot at Calumet, Michigan in 1979. Four large, welded metal brackets were placed at the corners of the gondola cars, allowing the logs to be piled well above the normal capacity of the cars.

Since plastic simulates metal very well, building these brackets would make an excellent beginning project for anyone just starting to scratchbuild in styrene. Any gondola or even a flat car could be used as the starting point for the project.

The entire project consists of cutting out a few pieces of sheet styrene, drilling some holes, and gluing the pieces together. Here are some step-by-step instructions (Figs. 17-3 through 17-6).

☐ Study the scale drawings and the exploded view in Figs. 17-7 and 17-8. Then lay out and cut out four pieces of 1/2-or1-inch styrene 15 inches × 9 feet with a 3-inch- × -3-foot cut out at the top.

☐ Using both a small and large drill, make a number of holes in the stock. There's no need to be perfect, since many of these holes were randomly drilled to attach chains or metal straps to hold the logs.

☐ From 1/2- × -3-inch or 1- × -3-inch strips (I used Evergreen Scale Models' styrene strips) at-

Fig. 17-1. The prototype braces are used to expand the capacity of gondola cars to hold pulpwood logs. This car was photographed at Calumet, Michigan.

tach the side braces, using just a little plastic cement or methyl ethyl ketone on a fine brush. To help align these small pieces, I placed the pieces against a heavy metal block on the bench (Fig. 17-9). Again be sure to use just a little solvent and gently slide the pieces after applying the glue to be sure it doesn't stick to the bench or the block. Also notice that there are two different braces: one facing left and facing right.

☐ Glue several loops and eyelets (Grandt HO-5085, 0-108) to the braces. I used eight on each one, but the number or size is not important. Looking at the prototype pictures, there are several variations and many broken ones.

☐ Finally the base is made from a 6-foot-×-1/2-inch styrene sheet with 3-×-1/2-inch strips along the sides. A plastic triangle acts as a gusset plate at the corners.

☐ The finished models are first coated with Flouquil "rust," then blotched with boxcar red, and finally washed with a black stain composed of alcohol and dye.

☐ The finished model can be glued to a flat car or gondola and filled with logs cut from dowels or garden trimmings.

I hope this first introduction to working with styrene has been enjoyable for you. Now for a challenge: for those of you interested in a special project in plastic, you might consider the log car braces shown in Figs. 17-10 through 17-12. They are a different style than those I've built but just as interesting. Dimensions are not critical; so just go at it and have fun (Figs. 17-3 through 17-15).

Fig. 17-2. A close-up photograph shows that the braces only follow a general design, with broken eye bolts and holes drilled at random places. I did not take any pictures inside the cars; so we can only guess about how they are attached. One thing is sure—they are good and rusty.

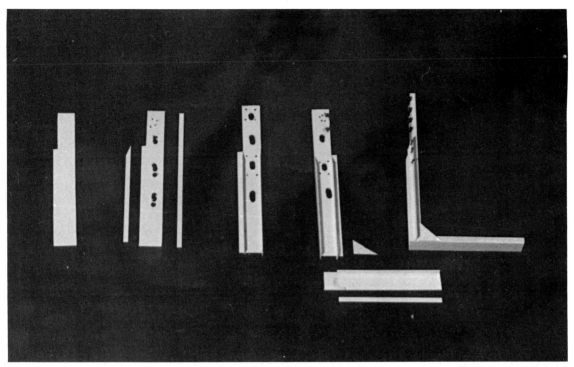

Fig. 17-3. The full construction sequence is shown from left to right. The base piece is notched at the top. Holes are drilled, with the larger ones being finished with a round file, and side pieces added. The finished upright with eyelets added. The base and triangular gusset plate. The finished bracket (bottom).

Fig. 17-4. The finished, weathered brackets show lots of weathering. Notice that there is a left- and a right-hand version.

Figs. 17-5 and 17-6. The finished model mounted in place will add an extra feature to your railroad.

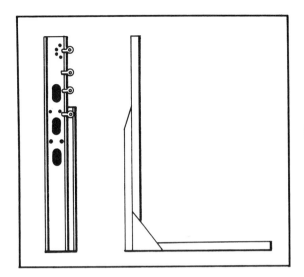

Fig. 17-7. Pulpwood braces (O scale).

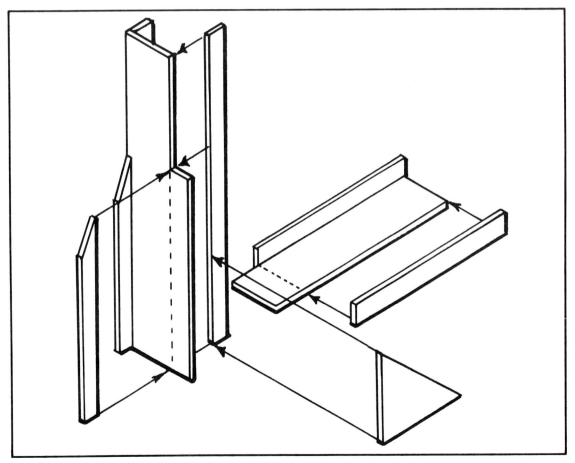

Fig. 17-8. Construction sequence (not to scale).

171

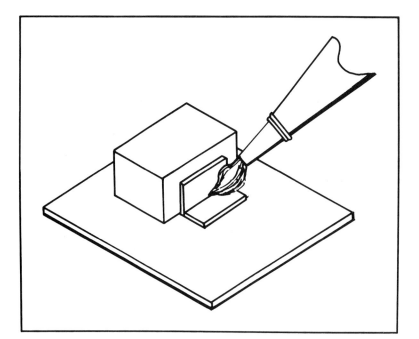

Fig. 17-9. Using a block for styrene fabrication.

Fig. 17-10. Here's a different style of log bracket that I photographed on the Apache Railroad in the White Mountains of Arizona in 1970.

Fig. 17-11. These brackets appear to be homemade, so there are virtually no critical dimensions. Everything could be formed from sheet styrene.

Fig. 17-12. Here's a slightly different version in the same string of cars.

Figs. 17-13 and 17-14. Close-ups show the heavy metal castings that could be formed from styrene.

Fig. 17-5. The rather crude cutting methods used on the homemade parts show that nothing about these brackets is perfect. If they were not perfect, why should yours be?

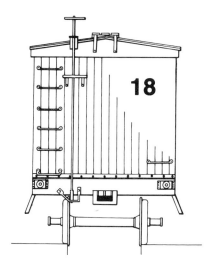

Building a Modern Soo Line Gondola

O NE OF THE FEW THINGS THAT IRRITATES me about model railroaders is the idea by some that scratchbuilding anything is beyond the abilities of the average modeler. Poppycock! If you've built a few kits and maybe a craftsman project or two, scratchbuilding should not be a very big deal. Sure there are more problems because you must provide the construction sequence, but heck there's a lot more fun, too.

As a project in plastic, I wanted to pick something modern, yet easy to build. In just the last few years, a group of investors has poured money into creating a national pool of boxcars called Railbox, and now a group of general-service gondolas called Railgon. The car we are building was made by the Thrall Car Co. in Chicago for the Soo Line Railroad in 1981. The all-welded construction makes for very clean lines and eases the modeling job. Although much of my modeling is of older-type cars, I was very pleased with this car, which required only one weekend to build.

☐ Begin by laying out the sides, bottom, and ends on the same sheet of styrene (0.010 in HO or 0.015 in 0) to ensure all are the same length (Fig. 18-1). Score and snap the pieces apart. Using 6- × -6 styrene cut 30 side posts. Again just score and snap carefully. Except for the four corner posts, all are angled back about 9 inches at the bottom with a razor.

☐ Using a fine brush and MEK, attach the corner posts and the center post. Use a square and block the entire piece against a wood stop. Make a spacer that is 3 feet wide and attach four posts on either side of center. The last posts to go in are 5 feet from each end and center over the trucks. Occasionally check with a square as you apply the posts. with MEK lightly applied the bonding goes very quickly (Fig. 18-2).

☐ Drill the two small viewing holes at the corners of the car and begin to put in the grab irons. I bent each iron from a small bit of wire over a metal strip to achieve sharp corners. To attach the irons,

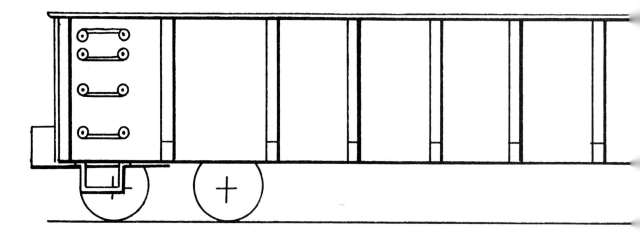

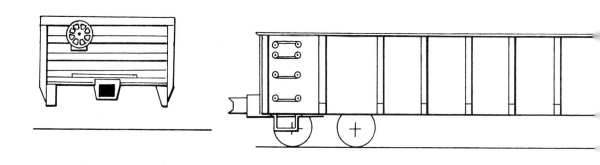

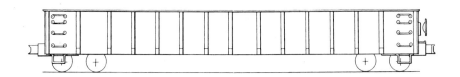

Fig. 18-1. Soo Gondola, side and front view O, HO, and N scales.

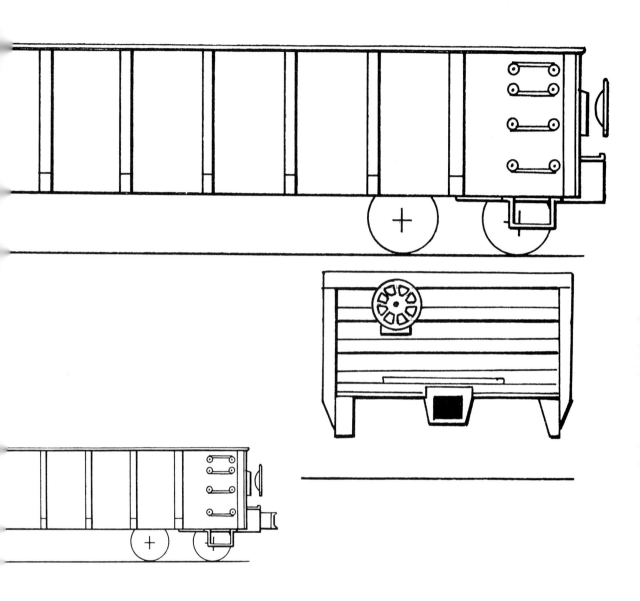

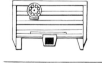

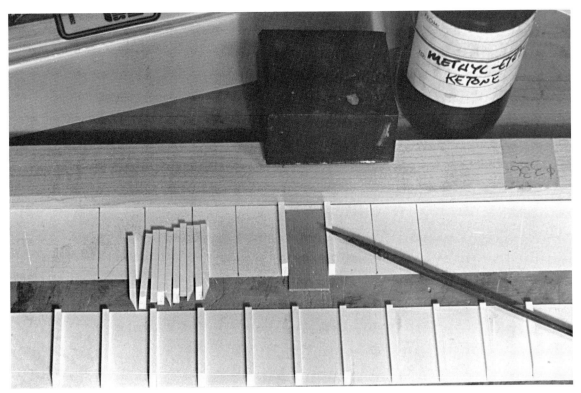

Fig. 18-2. The sides and ends are made from a sheet of styrene with small posts attached. Use a wood spacer and just a little MEK. Also push the entire side and each post against a stop, such as the wood piece at the top, to ensure a smooth top line.

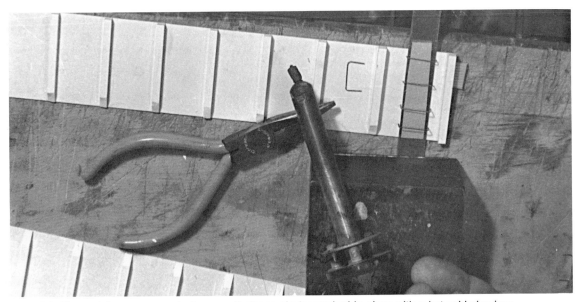

Fig. 18-3. The grab irons were made from small pieces of wire pushed in place with a hot soldering iron.

Fig. 18-4. The finished sides, ends, and bottom. Notice the NBWs at each grab iron.

I placed the same metal strip along the car side and held it in place with a heavy weight. I also added a wooden spacer to the left of the irons a little further away from the car (a total of about 3 inches). Now using a hot soldering iron I touched each grab iron and melted it through the sides. By carefully heating and reheating, the metal can be easily positioned (Fig. 18-3).

☐ A small NBW was added to each side of the grab irons. I sliced off the NBW flush with the washer, leaving no stem. Then just moistening the tip of a hobby knife, I picked up the NBW (that little bit of water surface tension lifts the tiny part) and placed it in a small pool of MEK next to the iron. The NBW quickly settles in place. Using normal tweezers is almost impossible for such a small item.

☐ The steps are plastic castings, although you could easily make your own (Fig. 18-4).

☐ The ends were made in a similar fashion to the sides, except a commercial brass brake wheel and housing were added on a small plastic pad.

☐ The couplers for this modern car extend far out on a special spring cushion. To simulate this, I built a simple styrene box around a regular Kadee coupler (Figs. 18-5 and 18-6).

Fig. 18-5. Construction of the enlarged coupler pocket begins with a box made of sheet styrene. Each side is attached with some overhang, which is then trimmed back to a perfect fit.

□ The finished car has metal bolsters to add a little weight, but even more was needed; so I added sheet lead to the bottom of the car (Fig. 8-7).

□ The entire car was spray painted boxcar red, and an extra heavy application of grimy black was dabbed about the interior with a little rust.

□ Lettering was done with Champ decals, following the instructions in Chapter 13. I couldn't find the exact decals for a gondola, so I used the boxcar size decal but from the next smaller scale; that is, HO for O, N for HO, etc. The fit was really good.

□ Finally the entire car was dusted with powdered tempera for that just-out-of-the-foundry-area look (Fig. 18-8).

If you need a modern car or just want to experiment with plastic select a similar car, follow our construction techniques, and have fun.

Fig. 18-6. The finished coupler pocket has a small platform added to the top, which includes two pieces of angle stock.

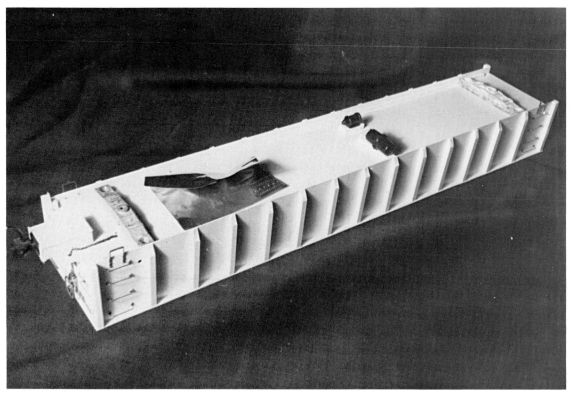

Fig. 18-7. The finished car has sheets of lead foil added to the bottom for weight. Only an AB-type brake system is needed here.

Fig. 18-8. The finished car is a proud model that would make a fine addition to any modern model railroad.

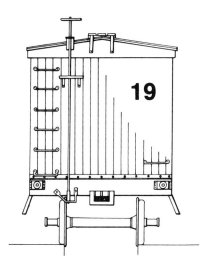

Finishing a Model

AN ORDINARY BOXCAR CAN BE LETTERED IN a hundred different ways. The lettering is kind of like your first name—it sets you apart from the rest of the crowd and is something special, very personal. A good lettering job can do wonders for a kit or simple model, while la bad lettering job will ruin even the best scratchbuilt model. Fortunately for model railroaders, lettering both as decals and dry transfers are available in an enormous variety from several commercial suppliers in all scales. Several suppliers (see Appendix) provide lettering diagrams or simplified drawings showing the placement of lettering. Using the guides you can page through tank car styles of the 1950s, perhaps, and pick out something that piques your interest. Repainted and relettered, a mass-produced kit or even RTR (Ready to Run) can can be as effective as a new scratchbuilt car with a small fraction of the effort.

DRY TRANSFERS

Press-on or run-on lettering has really simplified model car lettering. Lettering is applied to the back of a transparent sheet, which you can position in place and rub on the surface, thereby transferring the lettering to the car side. The surface is usually finished with a flat or matte finish that has a little tooth to hold the lettering. I like to use a small piece of tape to hold the lettering sheet in place while I rub with a blunt-nosed tool, like a ball-point pen top. Some people use a pencil, but the dark pencil marks tend to cover the lettering, making it difficult to see that the lettering is coming loose.

As the lettering transfers from the backing to the surface, you will see a definite lightening of color. After the letters have been transferred, lift the backing, trying to peel it back at an angle rather than up. The lettering should separate from the backing. If not, you may have to press harder. If only part of a letter transfers, push it down with your finger or a separate burnishing sheet, reposition the main sheet, and reapply. If the letter is not set in place, it may be accidently lifted by the sheet when you are burnishing another letter later.

Transfers are most useful for large signs and some of the elaborate old-time car "billboard" advertisements. Vintage Reproductions has some beautiful multicolored wall signs. Dry-transfer lettering alphabet sheets are available from any art supply house, and this is an inexpensive way to make special lettering for just a few cars. It would be most economical to use them for the large lettering and purchase "dimensional data" sets of the small lettering for the rest of the car.

Be a little careful with the commercial lettering sets, however. Most railroad cars use Railroad Roman or a similar extended style; that is, the letters are much wider than normal so that a person standing trackside will be able to read the lettering more easily, even with the very sharp viewing angle. Normal lettering would tend to blend together and blur.

Be careful with any additional painting and weathering since the thin lettering is affected by most solvent-based paints. I use this to my advantage by using a little solvent on a brush to spread and run the lettering down the side of a car or building. As transfers age, the adhesive becomes less effective, and the lettering may not transfer. If you just cannot replace an old transfer, try using a very light coating of a spray adhesive to renew the surface. Since you cannot control the coating as well as the manufacturer can, this suggestion is only for recovering nearly impossible to replace transfers. Even for the beginner, dry transfers are an easy way to apply lettering.

DECALS

The old standbys in the model railroad world are decals. Technically they are called decalcomanias, but I'll bet you've never heard any modeler say that! Decals from the 1890s to the 1980s are available from many sources in a variety of styles, road names, and car types.

Contrary to dry transfers, decals need a very smooth surface to adhere to. If the surface is the least bit rough, you may get a decal blush or haze that makes the entire piece of decal stand out against the background color of the car. To avoid this problem, make sure your surface is as smooth as possible and also coat the surface with a glossy (not flat) type of paint. Now I don't like to do my cars with a glossy surface paint; so I use a clear gloss coat just in the area of the decal.

The manufacturing process has changed somewhat over the years; so instructions will vary between decal types. The more modern types may be soaked in water for an unlimited amount of time, while the older ones have an adhesive on the decal that can be soaked off. Read the manufacture's directions carefully.

For older decals, I like to just dip them in water for about 10 seconds, then place the decal on the edge of the water dish and allow it to sit for about 60 seconds more. During this time, the thin film will completely loosen and can easily be removed and transferred. Next a small pool of decal setting agent like Solvaset is placed on the car where the decal will eventually go. The decal is placed on the wet area and positioned with the tip of a knife or toothpick. Many of the new decals are hairlike in thickness and can only be moved while the liquid film is present. With any type of decals, it is best to plan your positioning and move the decal as little as possible. Also trim the original decal closest to the lettering.

The liquid pool should eliminate any bubbles, but after the decal begins to set, any bubbles should be pierced with a sharp pin. A coat of decal setting fluid will soften the decal and cause it to snuggle down over rivet details and small imperfections. If the car has wooden siding, use a very sharp knife to slit the decals along each groove and apply the setting agent again, allowing the decal to fall into the grooves. Don't try to push them into the wooden notches, since the grooves will open much wider than the rest of the car.

Although some modelers say it is not necessary, I like to take a very fine brush and run a little of the base car color along the edge of the decal film—not around the letters since it is impossible to be steady enough, but just at the edge of the decal. This process forms a fillet at the edge of the decal, especially if you have some of the older, thicker kinds.

The final step is hide the decal gloss which, if not covered, will leave shiny outlines of every decal piece and clearly ruin the look of the model. Spray a flat, clear finish like Dullcote over the decal and most of the model if it has a gloss finish. As with any overspraying, test the coating on a side or place that does not show to check if the overspray is compatible with your surface. Add any chalk or additional weathering.

The entire process of decaling a car is shown using the combine from Chapter 2 as the example. See Figs. 19-1 to 19-6.

CUSTOM DECALS AND TRANSFERS

All along we've been saying how much fun it is to have your own special cars and models. Perhaps the ultimate is to have a long train of cars each lettered for your own railroad. Although it is possible to hand decal, letter by letter, a single car or two, the only answer to doing a multicolored herald is to have custom decals made for you. Decals can be made by printing on a special decal paper. You can make your own artwork, or many suppliers can provide custom design service for you. If you do it yourself, draw the lettering at least twice over-

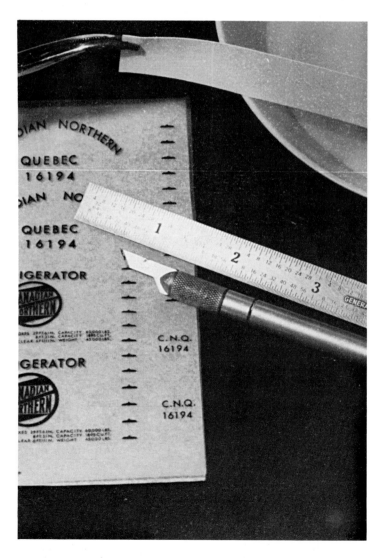

Fig. 19-1. The decal process begins by cutting out the decal with a sharp knife and metal straightedge, staying as close to the lettering as possible. The decal is then dipped in water for varying lengths of time, depending on the manufacturer.

Fig. 19-2. Next a puddle of setting solution is placed on the lettering location on the model, and the decal film with lettering is floated into place. Use a fairly blunt tool to position the decal. Should the solution begin to evaporate, add more since moving the drying decal will certainly tear it. The surface should be smooth and have a glossy finish. This car has four coats of paint, with sandings between each and a final clear gloss finish.

size with a dense ink like india drafting ink. Any special herald work should also be oversize, with each color appearing on a separate sheet. The manufacturers of these custom decals (Appendix A) can provide you with full information on making the designs. The cost varies, but $25 to $50 for a large supply is common. The costs are for printing entire sheets; so by packing as many items on a sheet as possible, you will save money. Of course, in the smaller scales, you can get more per sheet; thus they are less expensive.

Sometimes several modelers will get together to have different sets of decals grouped and made at the same time to save money on the camera and printing costs. Good lettering is the crowning touch to fine models. Practice and you can do a quality job.

COUPLERS AND TRUCKS

With the lettering and weathering completed, your model is nearly finished. The final pieces to add are the couplers and the trucks. Now I must confess that most of my modeling is for display purposes, not operation. I'm not ashamed to say that, because as we stated in the beginning of this book, model railroading has many facets that different people enjoy to different extents. So my advice here is limited, but I think important. Trucks and couplers will affect the operation of your finished models. If your trains keep uncoupling or derailing, your enjoyment of your railroad will undoubtedly decline. Although we've frequently stated that you can take liberties with dimensions and fittings on the models we've made, this is one area where precision will make the difference. If you really intend to do a lot of operating, then right now decide that the application of your trucks and couplers will be as perfect as possible.

The next decision to make is whether you will be using your equipment and yours alone on your

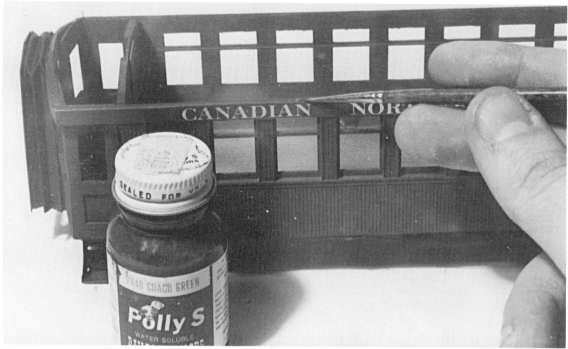

Fig. 19-3. Using a very fine brush, I like to fill in the open areas between words and at the edges of the decal film. Don't try to fill in around all the letters—it's just too hard.

Fig. 19-4. The finished lettering is given a coat of clear flat lacquer or other dulling agent. Be sure the spray and your decals are compatible. A final dusting with chalk will finish the car.

Figs. 19-5 and 19-6. Well, the car came out okay. I'm pleased to add this beauty to my collection. It took more than 6 months to build, with work in fits and spurts, but I think it was worth it. Don't you? Next time I hope you will be the builder.

layout or if you intend to operate on other layouts or share your layout with visiting modelers. This is not a decision to be taken lightly. Right now you may be a closet modeler or lone wolf, but things do change and in a year or two trading or operating with others might be very enjoyable. If you select an unusual coupler style or strange wheel flange depth, you may be out in the cold or locked into only operating at home.

Let's assume you take the precision route. What things should you do? First I suggest standardizing on one type of coupler. I use Kadee couplers on all my models and have been very satisfied with them. There are other manufacturers;

so I suggest that you discuss them with your hobby dealers. Many kit manufacturers recognize the modelers option here by offering kits "less T&C" (less trucks and couplers).

In preparing your couplers, take plenty of time to clean, file, and polish every part. The couplers must be moved by a small magnet in the track if you want automagnetic uncoupling, and the force applied is very small. Any tiny burr or rough spot will prevent the part from moving. A dry lubricant like teflon powder or the Greas-em sold by Kadee should be applied to all moving parts. Don't use an oil or grease; it will eventually pick up dust and form a gooey mass that will impede coupler movement.

Once the coupler draft box is assembled, test repeatedly that the coupler parts move with the slightest force and return to center. The couplers are centered by a tiny spring mounted inside the draft gear box. Of course with all tiny parts, the spring has a tendency to go flying off into never-never land at the tiniest provocation. Kadee has a new tool used to hold the spring and implant it without effort (Fig. 19-7). Recognizing the tendency of these springs to disappear, the manufacturers include one extra one in each coupler set. When I haven't lost it, I keep all those extra springs in a little bottle so I have replacements when needed.

Finally the couplers must be positioned on the car body. First they must be dead center and at the same height above the rails as all other cars and locomotives on your layout. Here is where we look to a national organization for standards that everyone can follow. The National Model Railroad Association has established standards or coupler height and position (Table 19-1 and Fig. 19-8). If all modelers would follow these guidelines, then interchange would be simple. You can buy or make a simple coupler height gauge by mounting a coupler on a wooden block at the exact height for your scale. When a coupler is mounted, simply roll your car up to the standard and be sure it couples and lines up correctly. If not, the coupler must be raised or lowered.

Lowering is not too difficult—just remove the entire coupler box and add a thin shim between it and the car body. Kadee sells small fiber shims, or you can make your own from cardstock or even thin

Fig. 19-7. Even if you have more than the average number of thumbs, you can put the springs in Kadee couplers with this tool.

Table 19-1. Coupler Height Data.

Name of Scale	Center of Coupler Above Top of Rail
O	11/16″
S	17/32″
OO	29/64″
HO	25/64″
TT	9/32″
On3	9/16″

metal. Again check and recheck the final fit.

Raising the coupler is another thing. You can put a shim on the truck and thus raise the entire car body. This method is tricky and can make your car look like a flamingo out of water if it gets up too high. An alternative is even more difficult, and involves cutting away a little bit of the floor directly above the coupler pocket, thus raising the coupler. The best practice is to design or buy your cars with the frame and bolsters properly aligned to minimize coupler positioning.

The newer couplers are all plastic, but some were made from metal, and you must be careful attaching them to metal locomotives or cars. It is possible, depending on your wiring system, to short out one car with another through the couplers. It's best to insulate all couplers. Good coupler mounting can become a habit, and when it does your cars will operate a lot better.

There are many choices of trucks whose manufacturers follow NMRA standards. More often than not, the problem of derailments lies in poor track construction rather than bad trucks. You can check trucks by using an *NMRA standard gage,* which is a small piece of metal with notches precision-machined at different locations to measure such things as track gauge (wheel spread) and flange depth. Too wide a gauge and the wheels bind; too narrow and they will walk out of the tracks. Too deep a flange and it may strike the fillings of turnouts and crossovers (Fig. 19-9). Incorrect wheel sets can be pulled or pushed into correct gage on the axle and locked in place with a tiny drop of ACC on the side face of the wheel. The NMRA gage can also be used to check every possible feature of track work and clearances around the track. It is an indispensable tool for every modeler, operator or not.

Clearances around trucks are another consideration with which we must deal. Prototype railroads have very large radii curves where the trucks do not turn very much. The braking system

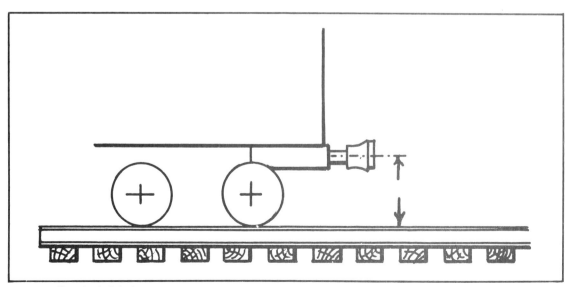

Fig. 19-8. Coupler height (not to scale).

189

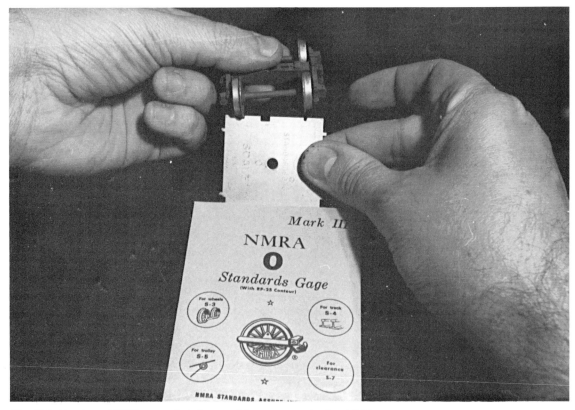

Fig. 19-9. Here's an NMRA gauge is being used to measure wheel spacing.

is connected to the trucks, and the many rods, chains, and support pieces that extend below the cars do not interfere. For models the trucks, do turn significantly because of the very sharp unprototypical curves; so you need to test that the trucks will clear the truss rods and extensions below scratchbuilt or kitbashed models. This is a point to ponder because it can be very disappointing to see your brand new scratchbuilt car bind up and hunch over while rounding the first curve on its maiden trip.

One other element to consider is the weight of the cars. Too light and they will pull off the track around curves; too heavy and the length of your trains will be severely restricted. There are some general rules of thumb. In HO, start with 1 ounce and add about 1/2 ounce for each inch of car length. That is, a 4-inch-long car should weigh 3 ounces (1 ounce plus $1/2 \times 4 = 1 + 2 = 3$). In S scale,

use 2 ounces as the starting point and add 1/2 ounce per inch. In O scale start with 4 ounces and add the same factor. Usually O scale cars do not need extra weight.

The weight should be added as low as possible to make the center of gravity close to the tracks. Some modelers place a sheet of thin lead or small lead weights, which can be purchased at the hobby shop, in the cars for weight. Others mix lead buck shot with glue and pour the mix into openings in the car until the correct weight is achieved. A very clever way to meet the problem is to coil ordinary solder around the axles of the trucks, thus putting the weight as close to the rails as possible. This is especially useful for open cars, such as flats or gondolas. Just remember that smooth operation may require some additional weights in your cars. Following these suggestions, you should have trouble free fun with your model cars.

EPILOGUE

You may have come to the end of the text, but we certainly hope that this is just the beginning of your interest in modeling, experimentation, kit assembly, kitbashing, and perhaps scratchbuilding as well. The ready-to-run equipment and kits are certainly a valuable asset to the hobby. They allow you to quickly develop a layout or mini rail empire. They make a fine basic foundation, just like the frozen food and delicatessen carry-out elements of a dinner. It always adds a special personal touch when you top off the basics with a special homemade dessert. That finishing touch may be something simple that has a special twist, or it can be something very elaborate reflecting hours of dedicated, careful work. We expect that somehow this book has given you a chance to kindle an interest in building those special models for your railroad. Nurture that spirit.

The ideas presented here are by no means the entire scope of our knowledge in these areas, nor is this book intended to be a definitive guide to railroad modeling at every stage. It is simply a start. Your skills are the total of the efforts you make—the mistakes as well as the successes. We trust you will build from this start and gain as much fun and satisfaction from model railroading as you can. Happy rails!

Appendix

Suppliers and Historical Societies

Suppliers

Check magazines for latest addresses.

American Standard Car Co.
P.O. Box 394
Crystal Lake, IL 60014

O scale craftsman kits.

Brookstone Company
127 Vose Farm Road
Peterborough, NH 03458

Fine craftsman type tools mostly woodworking.

Castolite Company
Box 391
Woodstock, IL 60098

Complete line of casting materials & supplies, latex rubber, RTV, plastics in small quantities.

Champion Decal Co.
P.O. Box 1178C
Minor, ND 58701

Extensive line of decals in all scales.

Chooch Enterprise, Inc. Box 217 Redmond, WA 98052	*Detail parts*
Coronado Scale Models 1544 East Cypress Street Phoenix, AZ 85006	*Small parts, scratchbuild-* *ing supplies especially for* *narrow gauge models.*
Craftsman Wood Service Co. 2727 South Mary Street Chicago, IL 60608 also 1735 West Cortland Center Addison, IL 60101	*All types of specialty woods* *(not in model sizes however)*
Evergreen Scale Models 2685 151st Place N.E. Redmond, WA 98052	*Excellent quality styrene* *strips, sheets and special* *shapes in all scales.*
Fine Scale Modeler 1027 North 7th Street Milwaukee, WI 53233	*Many fine articles on model* *building techniques—few RR* *models however.*
The Gould Company P.O. Box 463 Verdugo City, CA 91046	*Styrene injection moldings.*
Grandt Line Products 1040B Shary Center Concord, CA 94518	*Every kind of plastic com-* *ponent part possible; car-* *ried by most hobby shops.*
Hoquat Hobbies Box 253 Dunellen, NJ 08812	*S scale supplies and dry* *transfers - all scales.*
ICC (Indianapolis Car Co.) 6710 Hampton Drive, East Indianapolis, IN 46226	*Modular car components* *plastic parts.*

Kalmbach Video 1027 North 7th Street Milwaukee, WI 53233	*Home video tapes for model railroaders.*
Kappler Mill and Lumber Co.	*Available at hobby shops. Excellent scale lumber.*
Keil-Line Models Box 794 Park Ridge, IL 60068	*White metal castings.*
Mainline Modeler P.O. Box 5056 Lynnwood, WA 98036	*Craftsman caliber construction articles. Excellent prototype information.*
Donald B. Manlick 2127 South 11th Street Manitowoc, WI 54220	*Custom decals.*
MicroScale Decals Krasel Industries, Inc. 1821 East Newport Circle Santa Ana, CA 92706	*Wide range of decals.*
Model Railroader Magazine Kalmback Publishing Co. 1027 North 7th Street Milwaukee, WI 53233	*Major modeling magazine, cover all facets of hobby.*
Narrow Gauge & Shortline Gazette Box 26 Los Altos, CA 94022	*Excellent magazine for the scratchbuilder and narrow gauge fan.*
National Model Railroad Association 4121 Cromwell Rd. Chattonooga, TN 37421	*Monthly bulletin, local, regional and national meetings and groups. Well worth joining if locally active.*

Northeastern Scale Models,Inc.
Box 425
Metheun, MA 01844

*Excellent scale lumber
stripwood etc. Available
at most hobby shops.*

O Scale News
6514 North 11th Street
Philadelphia, PA 19126

*Specialty magazine for O
scale modelers*

O Scale Railroading
6710 Hampton Drive East
Indianapolis, IN 46226

*Specialty magazine for O
scale modelers.*

Rail Graphics
1111 Beechwood Road
Buffalo Grove, IL 60090

Decals & custom decals.

Railraod Model Craftsman Magazine
Box 700
Newton, NJ 07860

*Major modeling magazine
covers all facets of hobby,*

S Gaugian
310 Lathrop Avenue
River Forest, IL 60305

*S gauge magazine and Heim-
burger House Publishing.*

Vintage Reproductions
Box 7098
Colorado Springs, CO 80933

All kinds of dry transfers.

Walker Model Service, Inc.
5235 Farrar Court
Downers Grove, IL 60515

*White metal detail parts.
Custom castings service.*

Wm. K. Walthers, Inc.
Terminal Hobby Shop
5601 West Florist Avenue
Milwaukee, WI 53218

*Complete mail order hobby
shop. All scratchbuilding
supplies.*

Scale Models   *Fine detailed 1920's cars.*
Westerfield Novels
1404 Evans Court
Elk Grove Village, IL 60007

Ye Olde Huff-N-Puff Hobby Shop   *Kits. HO scale caliper.*
P.O. Box 53
PA Furnace, PA 16865

HISTORICAL SOCIETIES

Send a stamped, self-addressed, business-size, envelope to the historical societies listed for particular information.

Ann Arbor Railroad Historical Society
853 North Fourth
Chesaning, MI 48616

The Baltimore & Ohio Railroad Historical Society
P.O. Box 12578
Baltimore, MD 21203

The Boston & Maine Railroad
Historical Society, Inc.
P.O. Box 2362, Harwood Station
Littleton, MA 01460

Burlington Route Historical Society
P.O. Box 196
Bensenville, IL 60106

Chesapeake & Ohio Historical Society
P.O. Box 417
Alderson, WV 24910

Chicago & Northwestern Historical Society
17004 Locust Drive
Hazel Crest, IL 60429

Erie-Lackawanna Historical Society
22 Duguesne Center
Newcastle, DE 19720

Great Northern Historical Society
6161 Willow Lake Drive
Hudson, OH 44236

Gulf, Mobile & Ohio Historical Society, Inc.
Box 3382
Springfield, IL 62708

Illinois Central Historical Society
Box 157
Des Plaines, IL 60016

Illinois Terminal Railroad Historical Society
c/o A. Gill Siepert
Illinois Central College
East Peoria, IL 61635

Kansas City Southern Historical Society
9825 Bellaire
Kansas City, MO 64134

Katy Railroad Historical Society
6832 E. Mockingbird Lane
Dallas, TX 75214

The Milwaukee Road Railfans Association
Wendell Murphy
7504 West Ruby Avenue
Milwaukee, WI 53218

MISSABE Historical Society
719 Northland Avenue
Stillwater, MN 55082

Missouri Pacific (MoPac) Historical Society
P.O. Box 0
Camp Point, IL 62320

MONON Railroad Historical
Technical Society, Inc.
410 South Emerson Street Mt.
Prospect, IL 60056

National Model Railroad Assn.
4121 Cramwell RD
Chatanooga, TN 37421

National Railway Historical Society
3325 Sylvan Road
Thorndale, PA 19372

New York Central System Historical Society
P.O. Box 10027
Cleveland, OH 44110

New York, New Haven & Hartford Railroad
Historical Society
Box 122
Wallingford, CT 06492

Nickel Plate Road Historical & Technical Society
P.O. Box 10069
Cleveland, OH 44110

Northern Pacific Railroad Historical Association
18027 Clarkdale Avenue
Artesia, CA 90701

Ontario & Western Railway Historical Society, Inc.
Box 713
Middletown, NY 10940

Pennsylvania Railroad
Technical & Historical Society, Inc.
Box 389
Upper Darby, PA 19082

Railroad Historical Society of Maine
P.O. Box 8057
Portland, ME 04104

The Railway & Locomotive Historical Society, Inc.
46 Lowell Road
Westford, MA 01886

Reading Company Technical & Historical Society
P.O. Box 356
Birdsboro, PA 19508

Rock Island Technical Society
P.O. Box 100
Silvas, IL 61282

Santa Fe Modelers Organization
P.O. Box 284
Comer, GA 30629

The Soo Line Historical & Technical Society
P.O. Box 1126
Manitowoc, WI 54220

Southern Pacific Historical & Technical Society
218 Norton #6
Long Beach, CA 90805

The Southern Railway Historical Society
P.O. Box 4094
Martinez, GA 30907

TP & W Historical Society
RR1, Box 174B
Morocco, IN 47963

Union Pacific Railroad Historical Society
500612 Capitol
Omaha, NB 68132

Wabash Historical Society
3005 Soft Wind Trail
Ft. Worth, TX 76116

Western Maryland Railway Historical Society, Inc.
Union Bridge, MD 21791

Glossary

ACC—Alphacyanoacrylate. Extremely fast-setting glue that cures upon exposure to water in the air. Best for bonding nonporous surfaces. Extreme caution should be used since ACC will bond skin or eyes instantly.

ABS Plastic—A polymeric material made from acrylonitrile-butadiene-styrene. Harder and more resistant than styrene.

airbrush—A small spray tool for fine-spray application of paints and stains with compressed air.

back saw—Fine-toothed saw with reinforcing strap along top (back) of blade. Also called razor saw.

balsa—Lightest modeling wood; 7 to 10 lbs./ft.^{3} Easily crushed and broken.

basswood (American Linden)—Lightweight, closed-grain wood used for many modeling projects. Harder than balsa; it has a tendency to raise a fuzz when painted or stained.

bastard file—Grade of file that is somewhat coarse.

belt rail—Wood framing ledge just under the windows in a passenger car.

board and batten siding—Vertical wooden planking with small wooden strips, called battens, nailed over the seams between planks.

bolster (body bolster)—Transverse framing to attach the body to trucks.

Bristol board—duty paper board with soft surface. Sold in thickness based on weight in pounds.

buffer block—Wood plate directly above coupler to absorb shock and protect end sill.

butt joint—Wood joint where the end of one board is butted, or glued directly, to the second board.

caliper—Precision measuring tool for determining small dimensions between two jaws.

car lines—Roof formers inside car.

cardstock—General term for all laminated paper

sheet material; usually cut with razor knife. Also see: *Strathmore, Bristol board, museum board.*

casting—Making copies of an original by means of a mold and some free-flowing material, such as plaster or resin plastics.

center sill—Main support beams running the length of the car and in the center of the frame.

chamfer—To bevel or flatten sharp edges and corners, usually at 45°.

compass knife—An instrument for drawing and cutting circles, which has two legs with adjustable screw between. One leg has a sharp point; the other accepts a pen, pencil, or knife blade.

contact sheet—Unenlarged negatives printed directly on photo paper.

creosote—Oily liquid from coal tars used to waterproof wooden beams and piers. Simulated with black and gray paints.

double-hung window—Window with two sliding sashes that move vertically next to each other.

diorama—Small scene or portion of a scene usually modeled in great detail. Used by modelers lacking room for a complete layout.

draft—Slight angle on a master or casting to allow for easy removal.

Dremel tool—Tradename for motor tool. See *Motor tool.*

drybrushing—Process of rubbing paint only on the surface of a material without any flowing of the paint. A brush is dipped in just a little paint; the excess is wiped off, and the nearly dry brush is used to rub pigment on an object. Used for weathering.

end sill—Transfer wood beam at the end of the car.

engineer's scale—A ruler, usually triangular in cross section, divided into several multiples of 10 divisions.

epoxy—Two-part (hardner and resin) thermosetting adhesive. Very resistant to chemical attack. Good for bonding nonporous materials such as plastic to metal.

fascia—Board nailed vertically to the end of roof rafters; sometimes used for gutter support.

flash—Small, thin sections of casting material that has oozed out between mold sections.

gauge—The spacing between the railheads. Sometimes appears in common slang usage to denote scale; i.e., O Gauge. Standard gauge is 4 ft. 8 1/2 in. between rails. Narrow gauge is any track spacing less than standard. Common examples are 3-foot, 2-foot, and 1-meter gauges. Gauge and scale may be combined in a shorthand notation. On3 means O scale (1/4″ = 1′0″) with a 3-foot space between the rails. HOn2 1/2 means an HO scale model (3.5mm = 1′0″), but the rails are spaced 2 1/2 feet apart.

grain—The direction and arrangement of fibers in wood, cardstock, or stratified stone.

intermediate sill—Longitudinal sills between the side and center sills.

lap joint—Wood joint where two boards are joined, each being cut to one half its normal thickness.

methyl ethyl ketone—Volatile chemical solvent used to fuse plastic pieces together. Use only in well-ventilated areas, keep away from flames. Relatively slow evaporating.

modules—1) Small sections of model railroads designed for portability. Can be joined with other modules to form operating layouts. 2) Repeating patterns or designs.

mortise and tenon joint—Wood joint where a hole is cut into one board and the second is cut down in a tooth fashion to slide into the hole.

motor tool—Hand held motor driven drill with exchangeable collets. Can be used with drills, saws, grinders, sanding discs and other cutting and milling tools.

museum board—Paper sheet used for modeling walls. Laminated material, but same color all the way through so edges need not be masked.

NBW—See nut, bolt and washer casting.

NMRA—National Model Railroad Association

needle beam—Transfer beam to support queen posts and truss rods.

nut, bolt, and washer casting—Simulating the end of rod showing the protruding threaded rod with the usual washer and locking nut.

pike—Short for turnpike or refers to a layout and general railroad scene.

prototype—Original, full-scale practice or object. To measure a full-size car to be made into a model later is to measure the "prototype."

purlin—Longitudinal roof beam.

queen posts—Castings to support truss rods.

razor saw—Very fine-toothed miniature hand saw. A miniature type of back saw with a ribbed reinforcement on the top to stiffen the saw.

resin—Organic-type chemical-with a high molecular weight which will harden under the appropriate conditions. Generally not water-soluble.

ridgepole—Top roof longitudinal beam.

scale—A proportion in size. The most common scales are:

SCALE		PROPORTION
O	1/4″ = 1 ft.	1:48
HO	3.5mm = 1 ft.	1:87.1
S	3/16″ = 1 ft.	1:64
TT	1/10″ = 1 ft.	1:120
N	1.9mm = 1 ft.	1:160

scale lumber—small pieces of wood cut to the exact scale proportions as commercial building material; e.g. O scale—2 × 4, 1 × 10; HO scale—2 × 12, 4 × 4.

scratchbuilding—Making a model or item from basic material, such as wood, paper, and plastic, without the use of a kit. Engineering drawings are optional, and commercial castings such as windows and doors may be used.

scribe—To cut or scratch a mark or line. Scribed material has lines cut into it to resemble board joints.

side sill—Longitudinal beam running the length of the car at the outside of the frame.

single-faced mold—One-sided mold with a detailed flat back.

solder—Mixtures of metal which melt at varying temperatures with different degrees of hardness.

SOLDER	MELTING POINT	STRENGTH
Silver solder	high	high
Lead-tin (40-60)	medium	medium
Cerro (Bismuth solders)	low (about 212°F.)	low

Strathmore—Commercial name of high-quality hard surface cardstock or paper material. Supplied in various thicknesses based on plies. Cuts very cleanly with sharp razor or knife. See *Bristol board.*

stripwood—General term for small pieces of wood cut to exact dimensions, such as 1/32 × 1/16. Also includes scale lumber which are reproductions of actual lumber sizes in various scales: HO—2 × 4, O—2 × 10. Lengths range from actual 12″ to 2'4″, depending on supplier.

styrene—A polymeric plastic material available in thin sheets that is easily cut by scoring and breaking along the score. Gluing may be done by pressing two pieces together and flowing a small amount of the solvent MEK into the joint. The solvent actually dissolves a little of each surface then evaporates, allowing the surface to fuse.

super glue—*See ACC.*

truck wheel—Wheel sets and frames.

truss rods—Metal rods running the length of the car which can be tightened to prevent floor sag.

weathering—Process of painting, staining, or coloring to show aging, use, or effects of weather on a model.

white glue—A polymer suspension in water. Sold

in a variety of commercial names. Some forms may be sanded. Others peel rather than sand.

X-acto—Tradename used for an extensive line of modeling knives and tools.

zona saw—Tradename for razor saw. See *Razor saw.*

Index

Index

Edited by Suzanne L. Cheatle

Other Bestsellers of Related Interest

MODEL CAR BUILDING: Advanced Techniques—
Dennis Doty

Advanced Techniques takes you beyond the basic construction of model cars to restyling, customizing, and designing techniques. Parts swapping, engine wiring, installing brake systems, top chopping both late-model and vintage model cars, and making many other modifications to kit building are among the advanced concepts explained in Doty's second volume. An in-depth look at the emergence of model car cottage industries examines the influence of this burgeoning sector. 128 pages, Over 150 illustrations. Book No. 3095, $9.95 paperback only

WORKING WITH FIBERGLASS: Techniques and Projects—Jack Wiley

WIth the expert instruction provided by this guide, you can use f Building, flying, and repairing all different kinds of airplanes are covered in this guide. Safety guidelines are included and the author also discusses the Federal Communications Commission RC frequencies. This book contains enough technical information to keep your planes in the air and your equipment in good working condition. 160 pages, 80 illustrations. Book No. 3020, $9.95 paperback only

WORKING WITH ACRYLIC PLASTICS, Including 77 Projects—Jack Wiley

Learn to make practical and attractive items out of plastic—an inexpensive and readily available material that is amazingly simple to work with. Now with these easy-to-follow instructions and show-how illustrations, you can learn to create all kinds of useful and decorative items from acrylic—home accessories, gifts, jewelry, art, furniture, dishes, and more! 256 pages, 328 illustrations. Book No. 1959, $11.95 paperback only

MODEL CAR BUILDING: Getting Started—Dennis Doty

In *Getting Started*, the basics of model car building are thoroughly covered. Chapters include a rundown of the tools and materials you need, descriptions of various painting methods, and details on realistic finishing applications for both plastic and metal car assembly. A brief history, tracing model cars from the introduction of $1/16$-scale wood models in the '40s to large-scale models popular in the '70s is given. The making of a model kit, from the proposal stage to actual assembly and testing in the manufacturer's shop, is followed. 128 pages, Illustrated. Book No. 3085, $9.95 paperback only

REAL-LIFE SCENIC TECHNIQUES FOR MODEL RAILROADERS—Carl Caiati

"Using commercially available equipment and components, (Caiati helps you) create customized equipment that can't be bought." —**Railroad Model Craftsman**

If you're a model railroad enthusiast, this complete, step-by-step guide is for you. It opens the door to creating elaborate pikes that are accurate to every last detail! 240 pages, 166 illustrations. Book No. 2765, $14.95 paperback only

Look for These and Other TAB Books at Your Local BOOKSTORE

To Order Call Toll Free 1-800-822-8158

(in PA and AK call 717-794-2191)

or write to TAB BOOKS Inc., Blue Ridge Summit, PA 17294-0840.

For a catalog describing more than 1300 titles, write to TAB BOOKS Inc., Blue Ridge Summit, PA 17294-0840. Catalog is free with purchase; otherwise send $1.00 in check or money order made payable to TAB BOOKS Inc. (and receive $1.00 credit on your next purchase).